THE **OFFICIAL** GUIDE TO THE DIPLOMA IN

Hair and beauty studies

At Foundation Level

THE **OFFICIAL** GUIDE TO THE DIPLOMA IN

Hair and beauty studies

At Foundation Level

Jane Goldsbro and Elaine White

CENGAGE
Learning™

Australia • Brazil • Japan • Korea • Mexico • Singapore • Spain • United Kingdom • United States

The Official Guide to the Diploma in Hair and Beauty Studies at Foundation Level
Jane Goldsbro and Elaine White

Publisher: Melody Dawes

Development Editor: Lucy Mills

Editorial Assistant: Rebecca Hussey

Content Project Editor:
  Leonora Dawson-Bowling

Manufacturing Manager: Helen Mason

Senior Production Controller: Maeve Healy

Marketing Manager: Rachel Doyle

Typesetter: ICC Macmillan Inc.

Cover design: HCT Creative

Text design: Design Deluxe, Bath, UK

Illustrators: Oxford Designers and Illustrators
  unless otherwise stated

For product information and technology assistance,
contact **emea.info@cengage.com.**

For permission to use material from this text or product,
and for permission queries,
email **clsuk.permissions@cengage.com.**

The Author has asserted the right under the Copyright, Designs and Patents Act 1988 to be identified as Author of this Work.

British Library Cataloguing-in-Publication Data

A catalogue record for this book is available from the British Library.

ISBN: 978-1-4080-1798-2

Cengage Learning EMEA
Cheriton House, North Way, Andover,
Hampshire. SP10 5BE, UK.

Cengage Learning products are represented in Canada by Nelson Education Ltd.

For your lifelong learning solutions, visit **www.cengage.co.uk**

Purchase your next print book, e-book or e-chapter at **www.ichapters.co.uk**

Printed by Seng Lee Press, Singapore
1 2 3 4 5 6 7 8 9 10 – 11 10 09

Jane Goldsbro

To Alan for all his support

during the writing of this book

Elaine White

For my parents and my sister,

Jill, with love

Contents

CHAPTER 1 Look into your future

CHAPTER 2 First impressions count

CHAPTER 3 Looking good, feeling great

CHAPTER 4 Get ahead in hair styling

CHAPTER 5 Face facts

CHAPTER 6 Nailing it

Foreword

I am delighted that two people whom I have known and worked with for a long time have again joined forces to write this fantastic book.

Jane Goldsbro and Elaine White are also co authors of *The Cutting Book: The Official Guide to Cutting for S/NVQ Levels 2 and 3* and *The Official Guide to the Diploma in Hair and Beauty Studies at Higher Level*. They are authorities in their field and their input into the hairdressing industry is immense. Through their work with Habia they push forward the standards for hair and beauty education worldwide.

Elaine has over 32 years experience within the industry, including over 16 years as a hairdressing lecturer and course team leader. Her current role as Senior Development Manager for Habia has been pivotal to many developments by Habia, including the new Young Apprenticeship and Foundation Degrees. Elaine is a true professional whose exacting standards and dedication to her work have enabled her to focus on the end product with outstanding results.

Jane has over 27 years experience within the hairdressing industry, including salon management, educator and for the last ten years as Director of Standards and Qualifications at Habia. The commitment she has to her work is phenomenal. From writing standards, managing people and relationships with partners to international development, her wide vision means that she has an impressive ability to see the steps needed to achieve an end result. Jane's contribution to the hair and beauty curriculum has impacted throughout the world; as a developer of structured education she is very much in demand across all continents where her views are consistently sought.

Jane and Elaine were delighted that Joan Scott author of The Official Guide to Spa fame was able to contribute to this new book. I've known Joan for quite a few years, as an educator and a Habia forum member so was pleased to see Joan's specialist contribution.

The launch of Diplomas marks an important step forward in education. The Diploma in Hair and Beauty Studies has been developed with the help of employers, schools and universities and the combination of classroom learning with practical hands-on experience prepares young people for work and university. As well as broadening the options available to young people, the Diploma also brings a range of benefits to employers by preparing new recruits for the world of work and further training, giving them and the people who recruit them a head start on the road to success.

Alan Goldsbro
Chief Executive Officer
Habia

Acknowledgements

The authors and publishers would like to thank the following:

For providing photos for the front cover and title pages:

Main image: Hair: Karine Jackson Hair and Beauty, Covent Garden, London.
Photography: Andrew O'Toole.

Thumbnail images in order top to bottom (cover) and left to right (title pages):

- Hair: Michelle Thompson, Photography: Ernest Collins,
  Makeup: Louise Shipton, Styling: MTJ Styling.

- iStock/Izabela Habur

- Habia. Photography: Joachim Norvik

- Habia. Photography: Joachim Norvik

- Hair: CREAM Artistic Team, Photgraphy by Andrew O'Toole

- Habia. Photography: Andrew Whitton

For their help with the photoshoot:

Doncaster College

Habia.
Photography: Richard Keenan

For providing pictures for the book:

Alamy

Beauty Express

British Museum Images

Denman

Dr A.L. Wright

Dr John Gray

Dr M.H. Beck

Dr P. Marazzi/science photo library

Gary Russell @ The Chapel, Tunbridge Wells.
Photography by John Rawson @ TRP

Getty

Goldwell UK

Guinot

Habia

Hair by Chris Foster for Foss Academy, Photography Andy Kruczek

Hair by Reds Hair and Beauty, Sunderland. Photography by John Rawson @ TRP.

http://www.style-flash.com

iStock photography

Kay McIntyre, McIntyre's Salons

KeraCare

L'Oréal Professionnel

Marcus King, Hooker and Young. Products: Matrix

Mediscan

Michelle Thompson for Francesco group

REM

Redken

Saks UK, **http://www.saks.com**

Sanrizz

Sémhur

Shortcuts

Shutterstock photography

Simon Houston hairdressing. Location: Ballymena, Co. Antrim. Photographer: David Goldman

Sorisa

The Penn Museum

The Advertising Archives

Wellcome images

Wikipedia Commons

Every effort has been made to trace the copyright holders, but if any have been inadvertently overlooked the publisher will be pleased to make the necessary arrangements at the first opportunity. Please contact the publisher directly.

The Diploma in Hair and Beauty Studies

Qualification information

The Diploma in Hair and Beauty Studies is a new qualification that will give young people at school the opportunity to mix their school studies with work-related learning and experience in the workplace.

It will offer the learner a real alternative to the traditional learning routes, offering a blend of both academic and vocational learning, mixing general education, job-specific theory, background knowledge and selected practical experience related to hair and beauty. It will give the learner the opportunity to explore a range of related careers and opportunities.

The progression route throughout the Diploma remains open, so that learners can progress on to academic study, take a higher level of the Diploma, move into employment, take up an apprenticeship or work-related training or carry on to university.

There are three levels of diplomas that a learner can take:

1 Foundation Diploma

2 Higher level Diploma

3 Advanced Diploma

Below is a diagram to show how the progression routes within the Diploma, which is a preparation for work qualification, works and how a learner can transfer on to job ready type qualifications such as a apprenticeship.

Progression routes within the Hair and Beauty Sector

There are two distinctly different routes available within the hair and beauty sector for learners.

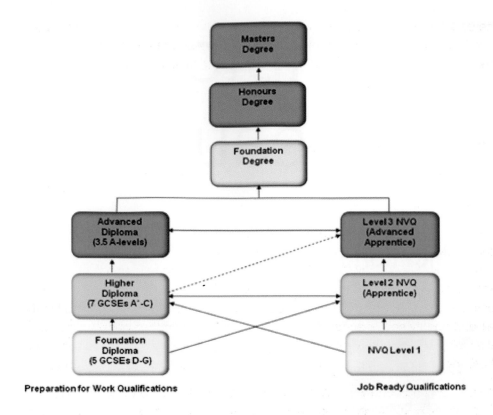

All Diplomas will include:

Principle learning – this allows the learner to look at the breadth of opportunities that are available in the hair and beauty sector as well as learning selected hair and beauty skills in a realistic learning environment across the six industries of hair and beauty sector.

The six industries are:

- **hairdressing**
- **spa therapy**
- **beauty therapy**
- **barbering**
- **nail services**
- **african-type hair**

Throughout the principle learning, learners will develop **personal learning and thinking skills**:

 Independent enquirer

 Teamworker

 Creative thinker

 Self-manager

 Reflective learner

 Effective participator

The personal learning and thinking skills include the ten employability skills that have been identified by hair and beauty employers as the key skills that businesses need new recruits to have. These employability skills are:

- Willingness to work
- Teamwork
- Personal and professional ethics
- Flexible working
- Customer care
- Positive attitude
- Self-managers
- Creativity
- Communication skills
- Leadership

This book is based on the Principle learning for the Diploma in Hair and Beauty Studies and within each chapter there are activities that will help learners to achieve both the employability skills and the personal learning and thinking skills. Without these skills it will be difficult for a person to succeed in the hair and beauty sector, and in an increasingly image-conscious world, the opportunities within the hair and beauty sector are endless. Successful people in their chosen field can take their pick from many top jobs – preparing models, working on magazines and photo shoots, in the theatre and film or even tending to the rich and famous.

The UK hair and beauty sector is regarded as the best in the world, giving plenty of opportunities for travelling and working internationally. To get to the top requires hard work and dedication. There are clear progression routes from trainee to manager or owner. The hours can be long and unsociable, but the rewards can more than make up for it. After all, how many jobs give a person the opportunity to be creative and try out new things every day? How many professions give you the chance to set up and run your own business well before your 30th birthday?

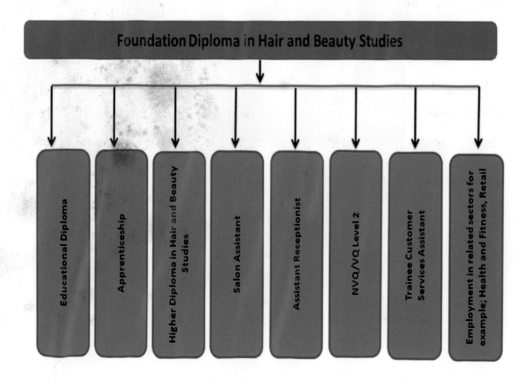

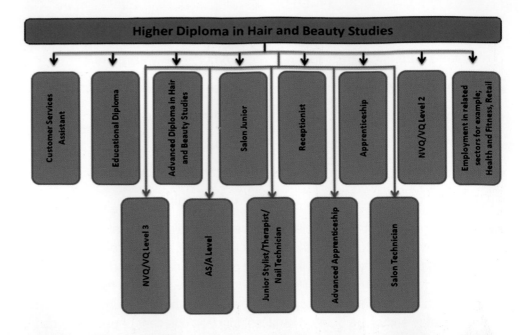

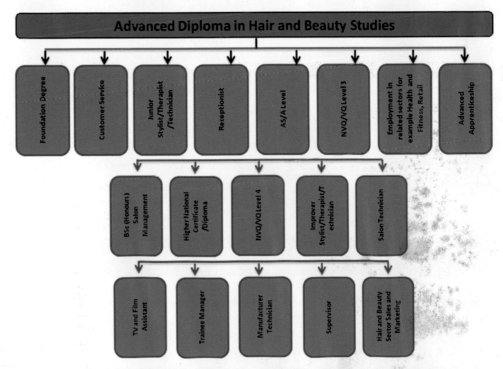

Additional or specialist learning – will allow the learner to choose options that will tailor their programme according to their interests and aspirations. This may include more hairdressing units, such as hair colouring or beauty therapy or nail units, or a learner can look at complementary areas that would enhance their career options that are outside the hair and beauty sector or take GCSEs or A levels.

Generic learning – encourages the learner to develop the broader skills and knowledge needed for learning, employment and personal development. This will include maths, English and ICT it will develop personal thinking and ensure that learners have a wide base of knowledge. These generic skills are often embedded in other aspects of the Diploma.

U2learn diploma

U2Learn

Also available from Cengage Learning and Habia: U2Learn Diploma

U2learn Diploma provides anytime anywhere access to a wealth of interactive activities to enliven and engage students at school, college or in the workplace. Theory as it applies to today's dynamic hair and beauty industry is truly brought to life, transporting students beyond the classroom into a variety of realistic and hair and beauty settings. Visit **http://diploma.u2learn.co.uk** or email **emea.fesales@cengage.com** or **sales@habia.org** to find out more now!

About the book

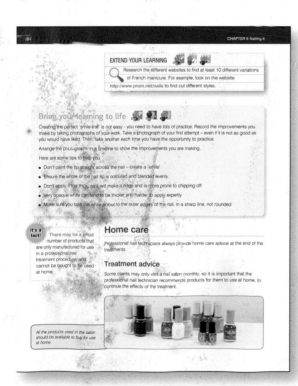

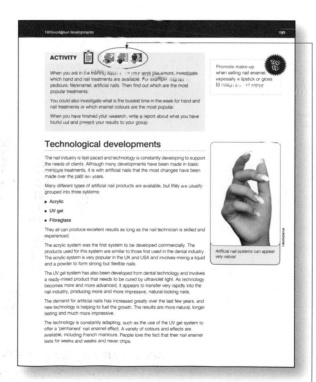

Extend your learning – Practical activities and projects will help you put your learning into practice and encourage further study.
Bring your learning to life is a feature that encourages you to use your skills in the workplace or in everyday life.

Activity boxes suggest exciting tasks that you can do with your classmates or on your own.
PLTS signposts show you the personal learning and thinking skills you need to develop as you work your way through the topics. These skills are essential to success in life, learning and work!

Top Tip! and **It's a fact!** boxes make information easy to digest and remember.

Step-by-step photos talk you through the basic skills and enable learners to visualise the processes involved.

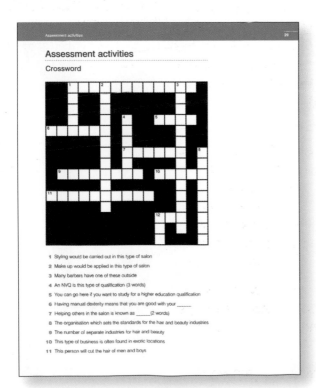

End of chapter assessments contain short answer questions so you can test yourself on the chapter subject and see how much you have learnt.

Crosswords and **word searches** test your knowledge of the topics and are fun and interactive revision tools.

Glossary terms are **highlighted** in the text and you can find all the definitions at the back of the book.

About the authors

Jane Goldsbro

A qualified hairdresser since 1982, Jane is one of the most influential educators in hair and beauty today. Her skills in developing the structure of UK hair and beauty education are renowned throughout the world.

Jane's early career as a hairdresser took her through a formative path where she ran salons and worked for some of the best companies and key influencers in the field of education, such as Alan International, and at Redken she worked as one of their top technicians.

At an early stage of her career, Jane was a regional winner of the L'Oréal Colour Trophy at the tender age of 17; this led her to start a teaching career at her local college. However, the deep-rooted commitment to continue learning saw Jane taking on her biggest challenge when she went to work at Habia.

In 1992 Jane began work at Habia as Development Manager for Hairdressing and within four years had risen to Director of Standards and Qualifications. This role saw her take on bigger challenges each year. Not only did Jane enhance the development of hairdressing education, she began to expand Habia's remit into beauty therapy. Since those heady days of endless development meetings, running standards workshops and training international educators in Habia techniques, Jane has still found time to develop her skills.

Jane Goldsbro

An established writer of technical material for Habia, Jane is also the author of two hairdressing study guides for Cengage Learning, the leading publisher in hair and beauty. As part of Jane's role, she is responsible for the content in the new Diploma in Hair and Beauty Studies. Her expertise in training and assessing has been picked up by well known awarding bodies such as City & Guilds and at the inception of a new regulatory regime by the UK government in training, Jane became one of the first inspectors for the Adult Learning Inspectorate.

Her role at Habia as Director of Standards and Qualifications now covers all six sectors of Habia's portfolio in hair, beauty, nails, spa, barbering and African-type hair. She is responsible for setting the standard for hair and beauty education from school leavers to university graduates.

Truly, one of the most knowledgeable hair and beauty educators in the world.

Elaine White

Elaine White

With a driving passion, Elaine White has expanded on her 30 years' experience in the hairdressing industry by implementing some of the most influential programmes within work-based learning.

Throughout her career, Elaine has been directly involved in researching processes and developing systems that have raised standards within the hair and beauty industry. She has contributed massively to the development of structures in UK and international hair and beauty education, which are renowned throughout the world. Throughout her career her passion for learning and development, not only for herself but for others, took her into the challenging world of further and higher education. Here she spent more than 16 years as an educator in both Lincolnshire and Nottinghamshire, before joining Habia in 2001 as Senior Development Manager.

Her role as Senior Development Manager allows her to work with a diverse range of stakeholders, encompassing employers, schools, colleges of further education, private training providers and universities. This has allowed Elaine to lead the development of innovative programmes including the Young Apprenticeships, Apprenticeships and Foundation Degrees, setting the standard for hair and beauty education from school pupils to university graduates. One of the most rewarding projects was to research the incidence of dyslexia in the hairdressing industry that culminated in presenting to an invited group at the House of Lords, the home of the upper chamber in the UK parliament.

This invaluable experience has enabled Elaine to develop and update education over all six sectors of Habia's portfolio in hair, beauty, nails, spa, barbering and African-type hair. Her knowledge and experience has been further recognised through her appointment as the standard-setting representative for the Apprenticeship Approval Group for England and Wales.

If this wasn't enough, Elaine is also an Adult Learning Inspectorate to Ofsted. Her passion for quality is paramount and clearly evident through her work.

1
look into your future

Adam Harris @ MG Martin Gold, Stanmore

A goal without a plan is just a wish.

ANTOINE DE SAINT FRENCH WRITER 1900–1944

Introduction

You have chosen to study the Diploma in Hair and Beauty Studies – congratulations! By choosing this qualification you will learn about some fascinating, exciting and ever-changing industries.

If you think you might want to work in one of the hair and beauty industries you will need to develop a wide range of very special skills. It will not be easy. The skills take many years to perfect but this is because jobs in the hair and beauty industry are important. You can make people feel better, without the need for medicine, look younger without the need for cosmetic surgery and feel more confident about themselves without the need of a psychologist.

The hair and beauty sector is made up of six, very different, separate industries. The hairdressing and barbering industries include a separate industry for African-Caribbean hair. The beauty industries are beauty therapy, nail services and spa therapy.

The hair and beauty industries are huge. They are global, with millions of clients worldwide. Welcome to the world of hair and beauty!

What you are going to learn

In this chapter you will learn about:

★ The services and treatments that are carried out in hair and beauty salons and spas

★ Career opportunities in hair and beauty and the links to other industries

★ The qualifications required for the hair and beauty industries

★ The career progression in hair and beauty

★ The pay you can expect to earn working in hair and beauty

★ The skills and personal qualities you will need to succeed in hair and beauty

★ What employers expect from those that work in hair and beauty

★ The size of the hair and beauty industries in the UK

★ The professional and trade organisations that support the hair and beauty industries

The treatments and services that are carried out in the hair and beauty industries

Hairdressing

As well as cutting and styling hair, a hairdresser provides chemical services such as colouring perming and relaxing hair. Colouring is done to change the natural colour of hair. Another chemical treatment is perming, where hair can be changed to make it curlier than it naturally is. Relaxing is done to make the hair straighter than it naturally is.

Barbering

Barbers work on the hair of men and boys. Their services include traditional hair cutting, clippering, cutting facial hair and shaving. Barbers also carry out face and head massage. Some barbers will also provide chemical services such as colouring and perming.

© Habia

Treatments taking place in a hairdressing salon

EXTEND YOUR LEARNING

There is a tradition for barbershops to display a red and white pole outside. Investigate the history behind the coloured poles.

African-Caribbean hair

There are many different types of hair, one of which is the African type. You can read about the variations in hair type in Chapter 4, get ahead in hairstyling.

In addition to hair cutting and styling, those that work on African-type hair will offer services such as chemical relaxing, which is a process that *permanently* straightens very tight curls. Styling techniques include thermal styling where hot curling irons are used to *temporarily* straighten hair.

It's a fact!

There is a growth in the number of salons which focus on *natural* African-type hair. In these salons, chemical treatments would not be used to straighten or change the curls in African-type hair. Instead, styling techniques are used that work with and enhance the natural appearance of the hair type.

A barber's pole

EXTEND YOUR LEARNING

During the 1970s there was a great deal of interest in Rastafari. This is a religion which developed in Jamaica in the 1930s. Those who follow the beliefs twist their natural African-type hair into a style known as **dreadlocks**.

Research the Rastafarian faith and investigate why the hairstyle is so important.

A hair salon for clients with African-type hair

Top tip

Try this website for your research http://www.bbc.co.uk/religion/religions/rastafari/ataglance/glance.shtml

ACTIVITY

Look in magazines or search for images on the Internet. Find some examples of locks on African-type, or mixed-race hair.

Beauty therapy

Beauty therapists provide treatments to enhance the appearance, well-being and relaxation of clients. The treatments carried out include manicure, pedicure, makeup, waxing and body massage.

Locks in African type hair

EXTEND YOUR LEARNING

Carry out some research and find out other treatments that beauty therapists offer to improve the appearance of the body.

Beauty therapy salons are very calming and peaceful environments where clients can relax

Nail services

The people that carry out nail services are known as **nail technicians**.

Nail technicians carry out manicures and pedicures to improve the appearance of nails on the hands and the feet.

Nail technicians also lengthen and enhance the appearance of nails with nail extensions. Decorating nails is known as **nail art**, where **stencilling**, **freehand** and **airbrushing** techniques are all used.

Nail art

A nail technician at work

A spa pedicure chair at a nail salon

EXTEND YOUR LEARNING

There are three different types of nail extension systems – gels, acrylics and wraps. Use the Internet or read about them in a textbook to investigate each of the systems. Write a short report about the different systems. If you have your own nails extended you could write about this in your report too.

A spa

Spa therapy

Spa therapists improve the appearance of the face and body and enhance health and well-being. One special feature of spas is that many of the treatments used are water-based. They include heat and wet treatments such as **hydrotherapy**, **flotation**, **steam**, **sauna** and **jacuzzi**.

EXTEND YOUR LEARNING

Investigate more about spa treatments by looking at the treatment menu of The Sanctuary, which is a famous spa in Covent Garden, London.

EXTEND YOUR LEARNING

Investigate the locations of some spas. Many are based in very luxurious and exotic holiday resorts all over the world. Then find an atlas and find the country they are based in. If you are interested in working in the spa industry you might work in one of the countries you have found.

Water treatments take place in spas

Floataway (www.floataway.co.uk)

Top tip

Use this web address http://www.thesanctuary.co.uk/pdf/The_Sanctuary_Treatments.pdf

Careers in the hair and beauty industries

Can you think of a job where you could be cruising in the Caribbean or starting your own business in your early 20s or working on the set of the next James Bond movie?

You can do all these things if you work in any of the hair and beauty industries. It is true that some of the jobs are quite rare and difficult to get, but this would not stand in the way of a hard-working and determined person.

Even if you are not interested in working abroad or being your own boss, you will find a great deal of variety in the locations of hair and beauty businesses – from the country to the city and from the high street to hotels.

Many hair and beauty businesses are small and employ fewer than 5 people. But, some employ as many as 50 people. In the large salons and spas it would be possible for you to work your way up the career ladder from a very junior position, right through to management.

Top tip

Look at this website for a holiday company that specialises in spa holidays in places such as Africa and islands in the Indian Ocean, in the Caribbean, and the South Pacific: http://www.kuoni.co.uk/spa/

Top tip

Download career leaflets for the hair and beauty industries to see all your career options. Go to the Habia website www.habia.org

Spas can be found in exotic locations

© iStockphoto.com/Quavondo Nguyen

Qualifications in hair and beauty

There are lots of qualifications designed for the job in the hair and beauty industries.

Learning pathways for hair and beauty

There are two different types of qualifications used for the hair and beauty industries. One type of qualification means you are ready for work; the other type is a preparation for work qualification.

Qualifications that prepare you for work

The Diploma in Hair and Beauty Studies is known as a *preparation for work* qualification. This is because the qualification allows you to investigate each of the six hair and beauty industries and shows you what is required to work in any of them. You will also be able to try out some of the basic skills that are required.

During the time you spend studying the Diploma you will also develop the **employability skills** that are required.

Qualifications that make you ready for work

One example of a *ready for work* qualification is a **National Vocational Qualification** (NVQs). NVQs are **competence-based** qualifications.

An assistant in a beauty salon

© iStockphoto.com/HannahmariaH

Because NVQs are designed for the job roles in each industry, they are assessed in the workplace for each of the industries.

NVQ Level 1

The NVQ Level 1 is for those that would like to work in an *assisting* role in the hair and beauty industries.

NVQ Level 2

NVQ Level 2 is designed for those that want to work at a *junior* level in hair and beauty sector.

NVQ Level 3

All those who wish to work at a *senior* level in any of the hair and beauty industries will be expected to gain an NVQ at Level 3.

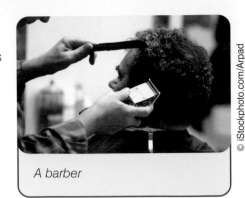

A barber

Gaining a ready for work qualification in the hair and beauty sector

You can study for a National Vocational Qualification (NVQ) through different routes.

There are no jobs at a junior level in spa therapy.

It's a fact!

Apprenticeships in the hair and beauty sector

As an apprentice, you will be employed in a salon or spa. During your employment, you will work towards an NVQ in the industry of your employment. At the same time as studying for your NVQ, you will also develop skills in communication, numeracy and information technology.

There are two levels of apprenticeship:

- **Apprenticeship**

- **Advanced apprenticeship**

Apprenticeships and Advanced apprenticeships are available in all six hair and beauty industries.

A college hairdressing salon

Apprenticeship

During an apprenticeship, you will study for:

- NVQ Level 2

- Communication, numeracy and information technology skills at Level 1

- Employment rights and responsibilities

Advanced apprenticeship

During an advanced apprenticeship, you will study for:

- NVQ Level 3

- Communication, numeracy and information technology skills at Level 2

- Employment rights and responsibilities

An apprentice hairdresser

College-based learning programmes

You can study for an NVQ from Levels 1–3 in a college of further education. During your time on the learning programme, you will spend some time with an employer on work placement. This gives you a true picture of what a commercial salon or spa is like.

It's a fact! Employment rights and responsibilities (ERR) is about learning about the rights and responsibilities of employment for you and your employer.

EXTEND YOUR LEARNING

Write to, email, telephone or call in to see your local training provider and ask for a **prospectus** of courses in hair and beauty. Investigate the options that would be available for you in your own town or city.

Bring your learning to life

If you get the opportunity to complete your work experience in a hair or beauty salon, ask the manager what employability skills they are looking for when recruiting a school or college leaver. Record how your own skills match up to those that the employer is looking for.

Higher education opportunities in hair and beauty

You can progress from the Foundation level of the Diploma in Hair and Beauty Studies to the Higher level, and then to the Advanced Diploma.

You can go to university and study for a degree in a variety of subjects. For example, progression from the Advanced Diploma in Hair and Beauty Studies can be to foundation degrees in subjects such as:

- Hairdressing and salon management
- Salon and spa management
- Spa and therapy management
- Cosmetic science

A graduation ceremony

© iStockphoto.com/RichVintage

Career progression in the world of hair and beauty

The table below shows you the progression pathways from entry level to a Master's degree. You can move from the bottom to the top in a vertical direction, or you can cross between the pathways.

Masters degree in salon or spa management	Masters degree in salon or spa management	Masters degree in salon or spa management	Masters degree in salon or spa management
Honours degrees in salon or spa management	Honours degrees in salon or spa management	Honours degrees in salon or spa management	Honours degrees in salon or spa management
Foundation degree in salon or spa management	Foundation degree in salon or spa management	Foundation degree in salon or spa management	Foundation degree in salon or spa management
GCE A levels	Advanced Diploma in hair and beauty studies	Advanced apprenticeship	NVQ Level 3
GCSE	Higher Diploma in hair and beauty studies	Apprenticeship	NVQ Level 2
Foundation Diploma in hair and beauty studies or NVQ Level 1 combined with GCSEs	Foundation Diploma in hair and beauty studies	Young apprenticeship[1] in hairdressing combined with GCSEs	NVQ Level 1

[1] Young apprenticeships are Level 2

Career progression outside the world of hair and beauty

You may decide that the hair and beauty sector is not for you, but you do like some parts of it. For example, you may enjoy the scientific experiments and research, the human biology, anatomy and physiology and the nutrition. In which case you may like to explore careers in:

- Cosmetic science
- Trichology
- Physiotherapy
- Nutrition and related areas

You may like to promote and or sell products, so you might consider a career in:

- Marketing or sales
- Customer service
- Retail

You could follow a career in nutrition

You could follow a career in sales or customer service

One day, you might like to be a manager. In which case, you could study for a qualification in:

- Management (salon, spa or other businesses)

- Receptionist

EXTEND YOUR LEARNING

If you have decided that *none* of the hair and beauty industries are for you complete this activity:

Investigate any of the alternative occupations that can be followed on completion of the Diploma in Hair and Beauty Studies. Find out what other skills or experience you need to enter them.

You could follow a career as a receptionist

What can I earn in the hair and beauty industries?

Some people think that if you work in any of the hair and beauty industries you will not earn very much money, but this can be said about many occupations, especially while you are training. When you first start work, you will not be able to do very much. So your skills, like your pay, will be limited. As you progress through your qualifications and take on more responsibility, your pay will increase.

The full happiness rankings

POSITION	PROFESSION	POSITION	PROFESSION
1	Beauticians	9 =	Engineers
2 =	Hairdressers	9 =	Architects
2 =	Armed Forces	13 =	Journalists
4	Catering/chefs	13 =	Mechanics/Automotive
5	Retail staff	13 =	Human Resources
6 =	Teachers	16	Call centre
6 =	Marketing/PR	17 =	IT specialists
6 =	Accountants	17 =	Nurses
9 =	Secretaries/Receptionists	17 =	Banker/Finance
9 =	Plumbers	17 =	Builders/construction

Many employers pay their staff **commission**. This is a percentage of the money taken from clients for the treatments and services. Therefore, the more clients you have and the busier you are, the more you will earn.

Although you need to earn money, job satisfaction is also very important. Hairdressers and beauty therapists have topped the scale for happiness in a job role.

It's a fact!

To be successful in salon ownership, you need to develop management skills as well as technical skills.

It's a fact!

The survey to find the happiest workers was carried out by City & Guilds[2]. Beauticians and hairdressers were at the top of the scale and secretarial, banking, insurance and finance workers were the least happy in their work.

Top tip

Check out the following websites for jobs in the hair and beauty industries:

- http://www.hairandbeauty-jobs.com/
- http://www.hji.co.uk/jobs/default.aspx

If you work hard and study for more qualifications you can earn high salaries in the hair and beauty industries. For example, managers and teachers in hair and beauty will be paid the same as those who do the same jobs in other industries.

You can also be self-employed or own your own salon. Then your salary will reflect the success and profitability of your own business.

EXTEND YOUR LEARNING

 Look at job advertisements for the hair and beauty industry. See how much salary is offered.

Could you be employed in the hair and beauty industries?

To work in the hair and beauty industries you have to be a very special person. You need to have an interesting personality and a wide range of personal skills. You must be prepared to train for a very long time and then to go on training for the rest of your working life.

For many of the hair and beauty industries you need to have a creative flair. For all the industries, you will have to learn about chemistry, human biology, physics, physiology and mathematics.

You must be an excellent communicator. Not only with your friends and the people you know well, but with people of every age, social and ethnic

---

[2] City & Guilds Happiness Index 2007.

A beauty therapist standing at work

background, occupation and gender. You have to be a good listener, be diplomatic and like working with people.

To find all these qualities in a single individual is very difficult. This is why people who have these skills have long and successful careers in the hair and beauty industries.

Standing and stamina

If you are considering a career in the hair and beauty industries, you need to be aware that it is tiring – particularly when you first begin. You may be physically fit, but having to stand on your feet all day is different to being at school or college where you spend lengthy periods of time sitting.

It's a fact! There are many competitions in body painting, nail art and for hairdressing. You don't have to wait until you are fully qualified to enter, as there are categories available for learners.

It's a fact! The nail service industry is the only one in which you will be able to work in a sitting position. This is because of the types of treatments and services that are offered.

Creativity and artistic flair

The hair and beauty industries are very creative. You will be able to design hairstyles by cutting hair. You need to be creative to apply hair colour and style hair. You can be creative with nail art or when applying makeup or body paint in beauty therapy.

Dyslexia

Some creative, successful and intelligent people in the hair and beauty industry are also dyslexic. Having **dyslexia** is not a barrier – in fact it is an advantage! While written communication may sometimes be difficult, dyslexics are often very creative. Dyslexics are also good at imagining 3D shapes, which is a very useful skill in the hair industry.

A hair and beauty competition

It's a fact! The D stands for *dimensional*. Hairdressers and barbers need to be able to visualise what a haircut or hairstyle will look like on the rounded surface of the head.

Colour blindness

Some people may have difficulties working in the hair industry if they are colour blind. When colouring hair, you have to be able to identify very small differences in natural and artificial colours.

Skin conditions

Chemicals, lotions and other products are used in most of the hair and beauty industries. Because of this, some people develop skin conditions such as **dermatitis**, especially if they have other allergies.

Communication skills

Clients will only go back for more hair and beauty services if they have enjoyed their experience. This means that all staff must have good verbal communication skills and enjoy working on a personal level with people from a range of different backgrounds.

Dexterity

You need to have dexterity if you want to work in any of the hair and beauty industries. Having manual dexterity means that you are good at physically handling things. Being dextrous means that you are able to coordinate the movements of your hands and fingers. You must be able to pick up and work with tools and equipment – some of which is small and intricate. You also need to be able to bend your hands and wrists into different positions to perform a range of techniques, such as massage movements.

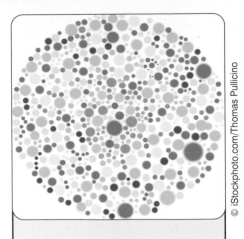

Colour blindness test – can you see the image?

© iStockphoto.com/Thomas Pullicino

Employability skills for the hair and beauty industries

Employability skills are different to the practical skills that are required to be a stylist, therapist or technician. Employability skills are important throughout your working life, but especially at the very beginning.

When you first leave school or college, the only skills an employer will be able to assess will be your employability skills. This is because you will not have developed any of the technical skills to work in the hair and beauty industries.

The employability skills you will need for the hair and beauty industries are:

- Communication
- Willingness to learn
- Self-manager
- Teamwork
- Client care

- Positive attitude
- Personal ethics
- Creativity
- Flexible working
- Leadership

Self-assessment for the employability skills required in the hair and beauty industries

Try this test to see if you may have the qualities of someone that could work in any of the hair and beauty industries.

Good at communicating

iStockphoto.com/Sandra Gligorijevic

Tick the A box or B box which is *most* like you in each section.

Communication

1	I only like to talk to people I know	A	
	I like to talk to anyone	B	
2	People think I talk a great deal	A	
	People like talking to me	B	
3	I am only happy when I am talking to others	A	
	I like to listen to other people	B	

Willingness to learn

1	I am curious and like to learn about new things	A	
	I am only interested in the things I already know about	B	
2	I try hard with things that take a long time to learn	A	
	I get bored if I can't learn something quickly	B	
3	I am not happy unless something is perfect	A	
	I cut corners if something takes too long to complete	B	

Self-manager

1	I am very organised and would know exactly where to find a particular item of clothing or textbook	A	
	I am not very organised and would have to search to find an item clothing or textbook	B	
2	I am up to date with all my school or college work	A	
	I have several pieces of work to hand in	B	
3	My friends often ask me to help them with their problems	A	
	I often ask my friends to help me with my problems	B	

Teamwork

1	I like to be in control of a group of people	A	
	I work well on my own and with a group of people	B	
2	I don't like to listen to those that criticise me	A	
	If one of my friends disagrees with something I am doing, I like to hear their views	B	
3	I don't like it if others do better than me	A	
	When I work with others, I enjoy seeing them do well	B	

Client care

1	If someone pushes in front of me in a queue, I would think of a reason why they had done this	A	
	If someone pushes in front of me in a queue I would immediately ask them to go to the back	B	
2	I like to gain feedback from others about work I have done	A	
	I am not interested in what others think about my work	B	
3	When I am in a situation where there is an argument, I do all I can to calm the situation	A	
	I enjoy getting in situations that cause arguments because it is interesting	B	

Positive attitude

1	If something does not work the first time, I am happy to try again	A	
	I get very frustrated if I can't get something to work	B	
2	I recognise that some criticism of my work will help me to improve	A	
	I get upset when I have worked hard and someone does not like what I have done	B	
3	I am aware that others may have a different point of view from me, and can still be right	A	
	If people do not agree with me, then they are wrong	B	

Personal ethics

1	I would hope that no-one would notice if I was late for school or college	A	
	If I know I am going to be late for school or college, I would always let someone know	B	
2	I only like being with people who enjoy the same things as me	A	
	I enjoy being with people who are different from me	B	
3	If I found a £50 note in the street, I would keep it if no-one noticed that I had picked it up	A	
	If I found a £50 note in the street, I would hand it in at the police station	B	

Creativity

1	If I have a new project, to complete I like to imagine how the end result will look		
	I dislike experimenting with different ideas and don't like starting new projects	B	
2	I enjoy trying new things	A	
	I prefer to continue with work that I know and understand	B	
3	I love to show others my new ideas	A	
	If I have a new idea, I like to keep it to myself	B	

Flexible working

1	I like to complete one job before I begin another	A	
	I am able to work on more than one project at a time	B	
2	I prefer routine	A	
	I don't mind if my routine is changed	B	
3	I prefer work that is routine	A	
	I prefer work that is challenging	B	

Leadership

1	When working in a group I am happy to give others tasks to do	A	
	I prefer others to tell me what to do	B	
2	When planning work I can see where one task can link with another	A	
	I like to plan one job at a time	B	
3	I enjoy helping others to achieve	A	
	I find having to help others frustrating	B	

Results for the employability skills test

When you have completed the questions, find out if you have the employability skills required to work in the hair and beauty industries.

Communication

Having good communication skills is probably the most important of all the employability skills. Communication is more than being able to talk to people you know well, such as your friends and family. If you work in the hair and beauty industries you have to be able to communicate with lots of different people.

Mainly As   *You need to improve your communication skills if you want to work in the hair and beauty sector. Being able to communicate includes listening as well as talking to a range of different people.*

Mainly Bs   *You have communication skills that would be useful for the hair and beauty sector.*

Willingness to learn

The skills, theory and knowledge you will study if you work in the hair and beauty industries are not easy to learn. They take a long time to perfect, and even when you have completed your early training, you will have to keep updating your skills for the rest of your working life. So you have to be *willing to learn*.

Mainly As   *You show the willingness to learn that is required for the hair and beauty sector.*

Mainly Bs   *The skills and knowledge required to work in the hair and beauty sector take many years to gain – and then you have to keep learning for the rest of your working life. If you are the type of person that is only satisfied when you can do a job quickly, then perhaps the hair and beauty industries are not for you.*

Self-manager

You have to be good at planning your own time if you want to work in the hair and beauty industries. If you are a good self-manager you will also be able to identify problems and then find a solution to overcome the problem all by yourself.

Mainly As   *You show signs that you are capable of being a self-manager.*

Mainly Bs   *You need to be able to manage your time and learning if you are going to succeed in the hair and beauty sector.*

ACTIVITY

Do you have good communication skills? Can you think of the times you have communicated well with other people? Perhaps you have had to ask for feedback from your teacher after a test or other school or college work. Once you have thought of an example, you will be asked to use it in another activity at the end of this section.

ACTIVITY

Can you think of an example where you have shown you have a willingness to learn? Perhaps you are learning something after school or college, or you have used research skills for projects or assignments.

Once you have thought of an example, you will be asked to use it in another activity at the end of this section.

ACTIVITY

Can you think of an example where you have shown you have the skill of self-management? Perhaps you are good at organising your own activities or are able to work under pressure.

Once you have thought of an example, you will be asked to use it in another activity at the end of this section.

ACTIVITY

Can you think of an example of where you have worked as part of a team? Perhaps you have been involved in an event at school or college, or taken part in team sports.

Once you have thought of an example, you will be asked to use it in another activity at the end of this section.

Teamwork

If you go to a busy salon there will be a team of people to look after you. There will be a receptionist to greet you and book further appointments. A junior stylist or junior therapist will prepare you for the treatments or services that are to be carried out by a senior stylist or senior therapist. Each person is working with others to ensure that you have a pleasant experience.

Teamwork is also about having respect and consideration for, and understanding of, others.

Mainly As   *Team work involves being adaptable and listening to the views of others. Perhaps you would be more suited to a career where you can sometimes work on your own.*

Mainly Bs   *You have the capability of successfully working in a team with other people, which is a skill required for the hair and beauty industries.*

Client care

How do you feel if you are kept waiting for an appointment without knowing why? Perhaps you feel unhappy, or uncomfortable. Client care is very important and can be anything from providing a full treatment or service to offering to make a drink for a client.

Mainly As   *You have social sensitivity and awareness, which is a useful skill for client care.*

Mainly Bs   *Having a lack of tolerance is not good when developing customer care skills, so perhaps the hair and beauty industries are not for you.*

It's a fact!   Client care is one employability skill that is linked to many of the others. For example, you cannot achieve good client care if you have poor communication skills or there are members of the salon team who do not work well together.

ACTIVITY

Can you think of an example where you have experienced good client care, or where you have given good client care?

Once you have thought of an example, you will be asked to use it in another activity at the end of this section.

Positive attitude

Because the training you need for the hair and beauty industries is long and sometimes difficult, you need to demonstrate that you are patient, tolerant and have a good sense of humour. You will have to deal with clients who may not always be as polite as you. So, you need to have a positive attitude.

Mainly As *You show that you have drive and commitment as well as tolerance, which are all useful qualities for the hair and beauty industries.*

Mainly Bs *You need to improve your skills of patience and tolerance if you want to succeed in the hair and beauty industries.*

Personal ethics

If you work in the hair and beauty industries, you will come into direct contact with clients on a personal level. Once a client builds up their trust in you, they sometimes talk to you about very sensitive subjects. You must never tell others about the personal conversations you have with your clients. You must be sensitive to their needs and respect their privacy.

Personal ethics is also about being honest and reliable.

Mainly As *You need to improve your honesty and reliability if you want to work in the hair and beauty industries.*

Mainly Bs *You show signs that you have a good work ethic and social and cultural awareness, which are required in the hair and beauty industries.*

Creativity

Being creative is a major advantage if you want to work in the hair and beauty industries. Being creative does not mean that you have to be an artist who can draw and paint. It can mean the ability to see *form* and *shape*, to *visualise* in three dimensions. You also need to be brave and experiment with different looks.

Mainly As *You have signs of creativity and the ability to inspire others, which is a good skill to have if you want to work in the hair and beauty industries.*

Mainly Bs *To be successful in the hair and beauty industries you must be able to share your originality.*

ACTIVITY

Can you think of an example where you have shown a positive attitude? You may have been faced with problems that you have overcome. Or you may have been criticised about some work you have produced, but you remained positive.

Once you have thought of an example, you will be asked to use it in another activity at the end of this section.

ACTIVITY

Can you think of an example where you can show you are someone that other people can trust? You may have a babysitting job, or help other people with errands.

Once you have thought of an example, you will be asked to use it in another activity at the end of this section.

ACTIVITY

Think of an example where you can demonstrate that you are creative. Perhaps you are good at art and design, or like to make your own clothes. Maybe you like to inspire other people.

Once you have thought of an example, you will be asked to use it in another activity at the end of this section.

Flexible working

The hair and beauty industries are not 9 to 5 jobs. Your work cannot end until your client is finished. You will not be able to have weekends off and you may be expected to work in shifts, which can include working in the evenings. You may also find that some times of the year are much busier than others. For example, working in a hairdressing salon at Christmas time is very busy as people want their hair doing for the party season.

Being able to demonstrate flexible working means that you have the ability to **multi-task**. When working in a salon or spa, you may often have more than one client to deal with, or have a list of instructions to carry out on behalf of a more senior member of staff.

Mainly As   *Your rigid nature will restrict you if you work in the hair and beauty industries.*

Mainly Bs   *You show signs that you have a flexible approach to work, which is an attribute that is required for the hair and beauty industries.*

ACTIVITY

Can you think of an example where you can show you can work flexibly? Perhaps you have a part-time job.

Once you have thought of an example, you will be asked to use it in another activity at the end of this section.

Leadership

If you can lead others you could have a very successful career in the hair and beauty industries, and the good thing is that you do not have wait until you are a manager to do this. Some leadership is required right at the very beginning of your training. For example, you need to show that you are keen to learn and then to keep on learning. Leadership is also about seeking new challenges and solving problems.

Mainly As   *You have qualities that can be developed into true leadership skills, which are required when working in the hair and beauty industries.*

Mainly Bs   *You need to develop you leadership skills if you want to work in the hair and beauty industries.*

ACTIVITY

Can you think of an example where you have demonstrated leadership skills? Perhaps you have helped and supported others.

Once you have thought of an example, you will be asked to use it in another activity at the end of this section.

It's a fact!   Completing the CV is another example of self-management. Self-managers have good planning skills, which includes planning for a new career.

Bring your learning to life

A curriculum vitae (CV) is a record of your personal details and achievements. Writing your first CV can be quite scary as you may have little real work experience to record. This can make your CV look rather short. However, employability skills are very important and are something that future employers will be looking for. Update your CV by adding a new section called **employability skills**.

Use the evidence from the activities in this section to complete it.

The size and structure of the hair and beauty industries

You will find hairdressing and beauty salons and barber shops on almost every high street in the country. Nail salons and nail bars are becoming more and more popular, and you will find at least one in most towns. You may not notice spas as much, as many are often found in peaceful, rural locations, in hotels or in leisure centres, rather than on the high street.

Here are some facts about the number of hair and beauty businesses in the UK.

In the UK there are around:

- 36,000 hairdressing salons, including around 300 that specialise in African-type hair

- 3,000 barber's shops

- 14,000 beauty salons

- 1,500 nail businesses

- 400 spas

And did you know that

- Approximately 260,000 people work in the hair and beauty industries.

Consumer spending

Researchers find out how much money consumers spend in the hair and beauty industries. In the UK, the total amount of money spent in hairdressing salons and on personal grooming is £5.25 billion. The spending for beauty therapy is £904 million.

In 2007, it was found that:

- A total of £161 was spent (on average) by each household in hair and beauty salons.

- A total of £171.60 was spent (on average) on hair products, cosmetics and electrical appliances used for hair and beauty. (Source: Family spending, *National Statistics/Marketing Pocket Book* 2007.)

Bring your learning to life

This is a whole class activity.

1 Each person in the class is to ask all the people who live in their house how much they spend on hair and beauty treatments each year. This means everyone – adults and younger people.

2 Total up the amount of spending for the household

Then, get together as a class and share the information you have all found.

3 Make a grand total of all the money spent in all the households for your class.

4 Work out the average for the whole class.

Is it more, or less, than the national average spend for the whole country?

Top tip   You can find out the average by *adding* all the money spent on hair and beauty treatments by each household and then *dividing* the *total* by the number of households.

ACTIVITY

Find out how much all your friends (male and female) spend on:

Hair and beauty services

- Hair services in the salon or with a freelance stylist
- Beauty treatments in the salon or with a freelance therapist
- Nail services in the salon or with a freelance technician
- Spa treatments

Professional products

- Hair products that are bought in a professional hairdressing salon or barbershop
- Beauty products that are bought in a professional beauty salon
- Nail products that are bought in a professional nail salon

Other products

- Hair products that are bought in a supermarket or chemist
- Beauty products that are bought in a supermarket or chemist
- Nail products that are bought in a supermarket or chemist

Compare the amount of money spent by females, with that of males. Who spends the most? And on what?

Hair and beauty industry and professional organisations

There are many organisations that provide support for people that work in, or own businesses in the hair and beauty industries.

Habia

Habia is the leading body for the six hair and beauty industries. Habia is known as a **standard-setting body** and is approved by the government.

Habia works with employers and other people interested in the hair and beauty industry to develop National Occupational Standards (NOS). The standards describe what is required to carry out the different job roles of a stylist, therapist or technician at different levels. Awarding bodies then use the standards to develop qualifications for hair and beauty.

Habia can also provide information on careers and training, and for employers they can help with the development of their business, employment law and health and safety.

ACTIVITY

Become a Habia member. It is free and easy to do online. Go to http://www. habia.org and then, membership. As a member you will be kept up to date with all the latest news about the hair and beauty industries.

Trade and professional bodies for the hair industries

Hairdressing Council

The Hairdressing Council is the organisation which is responsible for the state registration of hairdressers and barbers. The State Register began in 1964 when Parliament passed the Hairdressing Registration Act. You can become registered when you complete a nationally recognised qualification, such as an NVQ.

Salon Strategies

If you work on African-type hair, you may like the support of Salon Strategies. The orgainsation provides business training and support for employers in black and minority ethnic-owned businesses. They also promote outstanding performance

Habia logo

ACTIVITY

Research more about the Hairdressing Council.

You can learn more about the Hairdressing Council through their website: http://www.hairdressing council.org.uk

Top tip

Hairdressing Council logo

of individuals and businesses in the industries through the Ethnic Beauty Business Awards.

Trade and professional bodies for the beauty industries

British Association of Beauty Therapy and Cosmetology (BABTAC)

This trade organisation for beauty and holistic therapists makes sure that all members work to a strict **code of ethics** and conduct. They also ensure that workers are qualified and insured. BABTAC provide help for employers such as employment law, marketing research and information about the latest beauty treatments.

| SALON STRATEGIES |
| ... the business of beauty! |

Salon Strategies logo

Spa Business Association (SpaBA)

The association provides information and support for spa businesses, and also for students. The aim of the association is to provide one voice for the spa industry and it communicates with the government, the media, investors, legislative bodies and spa consumers. SpaBA supports the development of quality spa therapists.

BABTAC logo

Other trade and professional bodies for the hair and beauty sector

There are many other trade and professional bodies that you can research.

- British Institute and Association of Electrolysis
- Comité International D'Esthetique et de Cosmetologie
- Hairdressing and Beauty Suppliers Association
- Fellowship for British Hairdressing
- International Nail Association
- British International Spa Association

EXTEND YOUR LEARNING

Use a search engine and investigate the trade and professional bodies you are interested in.

SpaBA logo

spa business association

Bring your learning to life

You have now completed the chapter about looking into your future and you know about the career opportunities in hair and beauty.

If you have decided that a career in one of the hair and beauty industries would be interesting for you, bring your learning to life. Make an action plan about how you are going to get to the first rung of the ladder for your career.

The action plan should include:

- Your personal details – name address, date of birth

- The occupation you would like to aim for on completion of the Foundation Level Diploma in Hair and Beauty Studies

- The results of the employability skills test which you completed earlier in this chapter. For which of the 10 employability skills did you score well? Which need further work? How are you going to improve the score?

- How you would like to train for your chosen occupation – through an apprenticeship or through a college-based learning programme?

- What qualifications do you need to begin your chosen occupation? Perhaps you need to get certain subjects or grades of GCSEs, or progress onto the Higher Level Diploma in Hair and Beauty Studies.

Then write a letter of application for the next stage of your career. Perhaps the letter will go to a local training provider, or a college of further education. It may go to the head of year for the school you are currently in. In the letter, request a place on your chosen course or learning programme.

What you have learnt

- The services and treatments that are carried out in hair and beauty salons and spas:

  - Each of the six hair and beauty industries offer very different treatments and services

Top tip

Look at the Connexions website for information about job opportunities. http://www.connexions-direct.com/

- Career opportunities in hair and beauty and the links to other industries:

  - You can progress from Level 1 to a Masters degree in the world of hair and beauty

  - The career opportunities open to you are not restricted to the six in the hair and beauty sector. The skills and knowledge you learn for the Diploma in Hair and Beauty Studies can open more doors – in media, marketing, design, business management trichology, retail and much, much more

- The qualifications required for the hair and beauty industries:

  - There are ready for work qualifications and preparation for work qualifications

- The career progression in hair and beauty:

  - You can progress from Level 1 to a Masters degree in hair and beauty subjects

  - You can work from a very junior position to higher management

- The pay you can expect to earn working in hair and beauty:

  - The pay is low while training, but increases when you are qualified

- What employers expect from those that work in hair and beauty:

  - Employability skills as important in whichever occupation you choose to work in

  - Good communication skills are vital for the hair and beauty industry. You also need to show that you have, amongst other things, a willingness to learn, can work in a team, have a positive attitude, are creative and show leadership qualities

- The size of the hair and beauty industries in the UK:

  - The hair and beauty sector is made up of six separate industries – hairdressing, barbering, African-Caribbean hair, beauty therapy, nail services and spa therapy

- The professional and trade organisations that support the hair and beauty industries:

  - There are professional and trade organisations for each of the six industries

  - The organisations provide support, information and the opportunity for workers in the industry to meet and share issues and good practice

Assessment activities

Crossword

Across

1 Styling would be carried out in this type of salon (12)

5 Many barbers have one of these outside (4)

6 Makeup would be applied in this type of salon (6)

7 This organisation looks after people who work in the beauty industry (6)

9 Helping others in the salon is known as _____ (4, 4)

10 Having manual dexterity means that you are good with your _____ (5)

11 You can go here if you want to study for a higher education qualification (10)

12 This type of business is often found in exotic locations (3)

Down

1 The organisation which sets the standards for the hair and beauty industries (5)

2 An NVQ is this type of qualification (5, 3, 4)

3 The name of a person that carries out treatments on the hands and feet (4, 10)

4 This person will cut the hair of men and boys (6)

8 As well as talking, communication is about _____ (9)

12 The number of separate industries for hair and beauty (3)

Wordsearch

```
G F T T Q U A L I F I C A T I O N S S
F U A T N J G P C O M M I S S I O N T
S I N A E E J N S P G O K E S G L B A
G N F I X C M F I N I Y D D T O P E M
N O E P V Q H Y I R E H S K U C X A I
I I R A I E N N O M U G S Y D Y L U N
S T Z E F H R R I L A O A R Y J Z T A
S A Z X S A S S W C P N L S E A Y Y T
E C Z S E S R E I T I M I O S D R Y N
R I S L Z G E Y C T S A E C C A A J E
D N S I P N G R T I Y I N T U P M E I
R U L A P I A F D I T N P Y I R X V L
I M L N E L N C A R V N B A R B E R C
A M I W D Y A O M T I I E Z R D B V U
H O K A I T M L O F K A T R S E M I T
C C S X C S X L L T D F H A P H H U T
T J Q I U P R E P C U Z L N E P G T I
P N R N R E X G I G N O Q V E R A C N
E Q Z G E X A E D P N C W Q F G C F G
```

Apprenticeship	Client	Cutting	Learning
Barber	College	Diploma	Manager
Barbering	Colouring	Employment	Manicure
Beauty	Commission	Hairdresser	Massage
Care	Communication	Hairdressing	Nails
Career	Creativity	Leadership	NVQ

Opportunity	Qualifications	Stamina	Therapist
Pay	Salon	Study	University
Pedicure	Skills	Styling	Waxing
Qualification	Spa	Technician	

Multiple choice questions

1 The number of separate industries for hair and beauty is:

  a six

  b four

  c three

  d seven

2 A barber:

  a colours hair

  b cuts the hair of women

  c styles hair

  d cuts the hair of men and boys

3 Someone who does nail art is a:

  a beauty therapist

  b spa therapist

  c hairdresser

  d nail technician

4 The Diploma in Hair and Beauty Studies is a:

  a ready for work qualification

  b preparation for work qualification

  c preparation for hairdressing qualification

  d qualification for beauty therapy

5 Teamwork in the hair and beauty industries is important because:

  a working as a team keeps the salon clean

  b working as a team means you get the chance to talk to your friends at work

  c working as a team means everyone likes each other

  d working as a team helps the business run smoothly

6 NVQ Level 1 is a qualification for:

  a assisting in the salon

  b hairdressing in the salon

  c beauty therapy

  d nail services

7 A competence-based qualification:

   a prepares you for work

   b prepares you for exams

   c makes sure you are ready for study

   d makes sure you are ready for work

8 Someone who carries out a waxing treatment is most likely to be known as a:

   a nail technician

   b hairdresser

   c beauty therapist

   d spa therapist

9 To work at a management level in the hair and beauty industries you need to have:

   a an NVQ level 3

   b advanced diploma in hair and beauty studies

   c foundation degree

   d vocational qualification

10 SpaBa is an organisation for:

   a hairdressers

   b nail technicians

   c spa therapists

   d barbers

Match the service with the job role

Draw an arrow to the person most likely to carry out the hair or beauty service

Spa therapist	Colouring
Beauty therapist	Body massage
Nail technician	Thermal styling
Barber	Waxing
Hairdresser	Pedicure
African-type hair barber or hairdresser	Shaving

2

first impressions count

Tracey Devine @ Angels, Aberdeen

You never get a second chance to make a first impression.

W. TRIESTHOF

Introduction

First impressions do count. People will make a judgement about you within the first few minutes of meeting you, and the way you present yourself and act will form that judgement.

The way you communicate with others is very important when working in the hair and beauty sector. Professionals working in a salon or spa need to build *relationships* with their clients and team members so that they understand each other and work with each other effectively.

To become successful in the hair and beauty sector you will need to learn about the different methods of communication which include verbal, non-verbal and physical communication. You will learn how to use different types of communication to give a positive impression of yourself and to give clients confidence in you and the salon.

What you are going to learn

In this chapter you will learn about:

★ The importance of creating a good impression

★ The professional appearance of the salon

★ The role of the reception area

★ Communication and behavioural skills

★ Using verbal and non-verbal communication

★ Understanding how people communicate differently

The importance of creating a good impression

The hair and beauty sector is all about making people look and feel better. They come to a salon or spa for a number of reasons:

- To improve their appearance

- To improve their well-being

- To relax and enjoy the experience

It is therefore important that everyone working in the salon works together as a team to make sure that the client enjoys their visit. As the saying goes, 'first impressions count'. The way the salon looks, the way the professionals present themselves and behave all have an impact on the client's experience.

© iStockphoto.com/© Inga Ivanova

A spa visit

Digital Vision/Alamy

A nail salon visit

The client will start to form their opinion of the salon or spa from the moment they see it and walk in the door.

- Does the salon look clean and tidy?

- Does the salon have a friendly atmosphere?

- Were they greeted by the receptionist in a friendly and helpful way?

- Was their coat taken and stored away securely?

- Were they offered a drink or magazine to read while they were waiting for their appointment?

- Were they kept informed of how long they might have to wait?

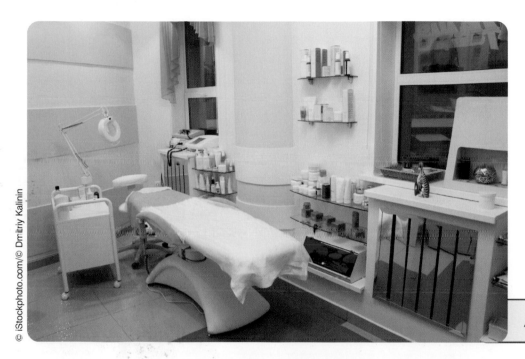

A beauty salon

EXTEND YOUR LEARNING

In a team or on your own, research and identify the main differences in style, mood and image between a hairdressing salon and beauty salon. As part of the project include information on the difference in:

- Layout and appearance

- The level of privacy

- The type of lighting used

- The volume and type of music used

- The services and treatments on offer

You can present your project in any format that you think will show you at your best.

All these questions will form part of the client's first impressions and all this is before they had actually started their **appointment**.

Professional appearance of the salon

The salon will reflect the **image** that the salon owner wants to portray to the outside world. It will influence the type of clients that will come to the salon or spa. Some salons are small and cosy while others may be big and more open plan. Some salons and spas will be found in isolated parts of the countryside, others in villages, small towns and larger cities. Some can be found in hotels or leisure facilities and on cruise ships. Wherever the salon is it will have an image. However, it does not matter what the image is, the one thing that all salons and spas will have in common is how clean it is.

A hairdressing salon

Courtesy of REM

Salon hygiene

Clients expect the salon to be clean. This means that during every part of the day it is everyone's job to make sure the salon is kept as clean as possible so that any client walking in the door will form a good first impression.

This means that during the day:

- Dirty cups and glasses should be washed and put away

- Floors and surfaces should be kept clean and any hair or spillages removed straight away

- Dirty towels and gowns should be removed and put away ready for washing

- Tools and equipment should be cleaned, **disinfected** or **sterilised** before being used on another client

- Used trolleys should be cleaned and prepared ready for the next client

Cleaning tools and equipment

A professional stylist, therapist or technician would never use dirty tools and equipment. They must be cleaned and sterilised before using them on clients. During your work experience and in your training sessions it is up to you to ensure that tools and equipment are clean and sterilised ready to use and that they are in good condition and fit for purpose.

Different tools and equipment are cleaned, sterilised or disinfected in different ways. There are three main methods of sterilising tools. These are:

- heat = the use of an autoclave
- radiation = the use of an ultraviolet light box
- chemicals = the use of Barbicide™

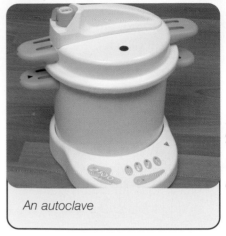

An autoclave

Courtesy of Sorisa

Heat

Autoclaves are the most reliable method of sterilising but are not always used in every salon. They are used for sterilising metal tools such as scissors, tweezers and cuticle nippers. They work by building up steam pressure and creating heat which destroys all living bacteria.

Radiation

The **ultraviolet (UV) light box** is often used as a method of sterilising tools such as combs, brushes, and nail clippers.

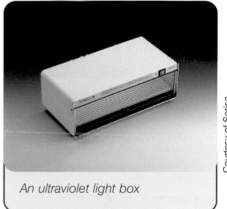

An ultraviolet light box

Courtesy of Sorisa

The tools must be washed and dried before placing them in the box. The ultraviolet light will prevent bacteria growth on the tools but complete sterilisation is not guaranteed as tools will only be sterilised on the areas where the UV rays reach, so the tools must be turned over to ensure they have been exposed to the light on all sides. Because this method of sterilising is time-consuming and sterilisation can not be guaranteed it is often better to use the UV light box as a hygienic method of storing tools that have already been sterilised by another method rather than storing them in your toolbag.

Chemicals

The use of chemicals is the most common method in the salon to disinfect tools and equipment such as eyebrow tweezers and combs. In the hair and beauty sector we tend to use a chemical called **Barbicide™**, a clear blue low-level disinfectant. It does not sterilise tools but reduces the probability of infection. Barbicide™ must be changed daily and all the tools must be totally submerged in the solution and left in the solution for the time recommended by the manufacturer.

A Barbicide™ jar

Courtesy of Sorisa

Electrical tools and equipment should be wiped down to remove any **debris** or dirt after and before use and then stored correctly.

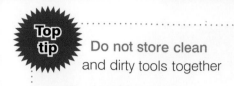
Do not store clean and dirty tools together

Always follow the manufacturer's instructions for cleaning and storing tools and equipment.

EXTEND YOUR LEARNING

Investigate how to use Barbicide™. Try this website for Barbicide
http://www.king-research.com/

When you have read all about the product, you can do the Barbicide™ quiz

Health and safety legislation

Health and safety is for everyone. There is **legislation** for all aspects of safety when people are at work. The Health and Safety at Work Act (1974) sets down the requirements that everyone must follow when they are working. There are sections that apply to the employer and there are sections that apply to an employee.

It does not matter what role or position people have in a job, everyone needs to take *responsibility* for how they behave and the actions they take. Everyone is responsible for their own actions, what they do and how that may affect others. Health and safety regulations and **policies** will ensure that everyone is aware of their own responsibilities for health and safety at work. Not following health and safety can lead to:

- Accidents in the salon

- Dirty and unhygienic tools and equipment being used

- Unsafe use and storage of products, tools and equipment

- Injury to yourself or other people

EXTEND YOUR LEARNING

Working in a team, find out as much as you can about the main health and safety legislation that must be followed within the hair and beauty sector. These will include:

- The Health and Safety at Work Act 1974:
  - Sets down the requirements that everyone must follow when they are working.
- Control of Substances Hazardous to Health (COSHH) Regulations 1999:
  - Covers the safe handling, storing and use of hazardous products
- Personal Protective Equipment (PPE) at Work Regulations 1992:
  - Special items of protective clothing that should be used
- Workplace (Health, Safety and Welfare) Regulations 1992:
  - Code of practice for maintaining a safe, secure working environment
- Manual Handling Operations Regulations 1992:
  - Safety procedures for manually lifting objects
- Electricity at Work Regulations 1989:
  - Safety procedures for maintaining electrical equipment

ACTIVITY

You can find out more about health and safety from the Health and Safety Executive (HSE) website: http://www.hse.gov.uk

Once you have gathered the information, design a leaflet, poster or mood board to present your findings.

The role of the reception area

The reception area of any business is likely to be the first area that visitors are likely to see. Because of this, reception must provide a positive and lasting impression. Most reception areas have a desk where reception stationery and equipment is kept. The desk must always be clean and tidy.

There will often be a waiting area for visitors to sit. The seating area must be clean and comfortable. Any reading materials such as magazines must be up to date and in good condition

ACTIVITY

Create a hairstyle, nail or beauty treatment file that could be kept in a reception area. The file should be of a good standard so that waiting clients can look at it to get ideas and inspiration.

Courtesy of REM

A reception area

The reception area is often used to display products and sometimes equipment for clients to buy. The displays must be kept tidy and free from dust. Attractive displays can be used to promote products.

ACTIVITY

Working in a team, design a promotional poster and then create a display using hair and beauty products that could be used in a reception area.

ACTIVITY

Most hair and beauty reception areas are visible from the street, so when you walk past look to see if a client would gain a good impression about the salon by looking at the reception area? Is the reception area clean? Does the receptionist give a positive first impression? Compare several salon reception areas and write a short report of your findings.

The role of a receptionist

The receptionist's role can be very interesting as they will meet a range of new people every day. The role is not restricted to the hair and beauty sector. Receptionists operate in other sectors, such as medicine, in hospitals and doctor's surgeries. You will also find receptionists in many offices and schools.

ACTIVITY

Make a list of the different places where a receptionist can be found. Can you identify if there are any differences in their job activities?

Receptionists are the first point of contact either face to face, or by telephone. Because of this they have to make a good first impression, both for themselves and for the business. Receptionists will answer the telephone, deal with enquiries, take messages, and greet and assist clients and visitors.

The skills of the receptionist

As the first point of contact receptionists must be confident, friendly and have a suitable personality for the business they work in. Some receptionists will work in a calm, quiet environment such as a beauty salon, others in a busy bustling environment such as a hair salon. They have to be good organisers as they have to manage time and work schedules for themselves and for other people.

Communication skills are very important for receptionists. This will include **verbal** and **non-verbal communication** as well as written communication. More and more receptionists have to use information technology as part of their daily work, so computer skills are also required.

Many receptionists will look after client information that is stored on a database or on paper records. In the hair and beauty sector records of client details are kept. They will give information on the services or treatments that the client has previously had, as well as personal details. It is important that these records are kept confidential and stored away correctly and securely, so that they are not left for others to read.

It's a fact!

The Data Protection Act is designed to protect a person's right to privacy and confidentiality.

Receptionists for the hair and beauty sector

Salons and spas that are large enough will have a dedicated receptionist. Small salons would not and everyone in the salon will be expected to make a contribution to the role. However, this does not mean that the reception role is less important.

The job role for a receptionist in the hair and beauty industry will include the following:

- Creating a positive and lasting impression of the business
- Handling client enquiries
- Being the first person to deal with problems
- Communicating with clients and visitors to the salon or spa, face to face, by telephone or electronic means such as email, and sometimes SMS
- Ensuring the waiting area is clean, well-maintained, safe and secure
- Taking responsibility for client payments by cash, credit and debit cards, cheques and vouchers
- Meeting and greeting clients and visitors to the salon or spa
- Making appointments
- Assisting clients with retail sales
- Displaying and promoting salon and spa products, services and treatments
- Monitoring stock by stock rotation
- Ordering stock
- Liaising with product manufacturers and their representatives

A receptionist answering the telephone

Answering the telephone

A receptionist will answer most, if not all the calls that are received by the salon. However, if there is not a receptionist, it is important for all staff to be trained in the skill of using the telephone.

The *tone of voice* that is used to answer the telephone is as important as body language for a face-to-face greeting. The procedure used when answering the telephone should be the same for everyone and the sound of the voice should be welcoming. When speaking on the telephone, a receptionist will ensure that they speak clearly. They will ensure that they do not mumble or speak too fast and will alter the tone of their voice so that they always sound interested in the caller's enquiry.

Taking messages

Receptionists will often take, record and pass on messages. Message-taking is a form of communication and must be completed clearly and accurately in order to maintain effective communication within the salon or spa. It is important to make sure that the message is only given to the person that it is meant for.

Messages must be clearly written and include, as a minimum, the following information:

- Who the message is for

- Who has taken the message

- The date and time the message was taken

- What the message is

- Any action required

- If the message is urgent

- How to reply to the message (contact telephone number, address, email)

Top tip Smiling when answering the telephone will result in friendly tone of voice.

ACTIVITY

Role play the following activities that take place at a reception area:

- Answering the telephone.

- Taking a message.

How did you deal with each activity?

Bring your learning to life

When you are on your work placement or in a salon environment, watch a receptionist at work. List the types of jobs that they do each day. Are there jobs that you think you could carry out now? Which jobs do you think you need more training and practice in? Discuss this with your teacher and together agree an action plan that you can follow to improve your skills.

Communication and behavioural skills

Communication is the passing on of information, ideas or feelings. How we do this and the way we do it will affect our relationships with other people. There are different methods of communication and it is important that you use all of them to make sure that people understand clearly what you are saying.

Verbal communication

Verbal communication is about talking and how you use your voice to get information across. One-to-one communication is an important skill within the hair and beauty sector. Your voice can expose your **attitude** and your **emotions**. A client will quickly identify your interest in them by the way you speak, through the tone of your voice and what you say.

To communicate effectively you should:

- Keep information straightforward and simple

- Speak clearly

- Vary voice tone, pitch and volume

- Speak with courtesy and confidence

- Use professional words and not slang

- Never speak while you are eating or chewing gum

Non-verbal communication

There are many forms of non-verbal communication, the majority of which professionals will use every day whilst at work in the salon or spa. These may include such things as:

- Making an appointment or writing down a message

- Gestures and facial expressions

- Eye contact

- Clothes and accessories

Top tip

Never use a **condescending** voice tone as this will make people feel uncomfortable and annoyed.

Pie chart of the way your communication is conveyed to your clients

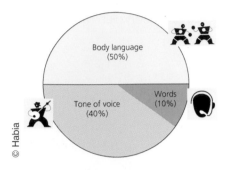

© Habia

When you are visually communicating with people your message is delivered in three ways: by body language, your tone of voice, and the words you say.

Your **body language** will account for approximately 50% of the information a person will receive. Your tone of voice will be approximately 40% of the information received and the words you use will make up the remaining 10%.

Body language is a very important part of communication. The way you stand, make eye contact and your use of facial expressions will give a message to people about you, about your attitude and emotions. For example:

- A genuine smile lights up your face and conveys happiness and interest
- Eye contact lets people know you are listening and interested in them
- Your head tilted to one side will indicate that you are interested

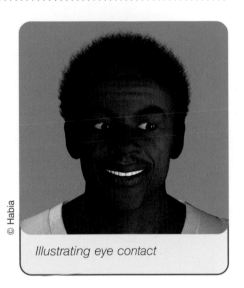

© Habia

Illustrating eye contact

© Habia

A person with their head tilted to one side

© Habia

A person with their hands on hips

Whereas:

- Standing with hands on your hips can give the interpretation of aggression
- Crossing your arms can make you appear defensive

Usually in the hair and beauty sector, if a client's body frame is loose or more widely spread they are generally more relaxed or at ease.

However, if a client holds their body in a stiffer, rigid or more uptight position they are usually experiencing nervousness, tension or discomfort. For example:

- A client touching their face usually indicates anxiety
- A client clenching their fist indicates tension or aggression

Being able to interpret these *signals* and act on them to reassure or relax a client will help to create a good relationship.

Clothing, jewellery and accessories are also forms of non-verbal communication. The moment you look at the person, you take in information about their *appearance*, the *clothes* they are wearing, the type of *jewellery* or *accessories*.

© Habia

A person with a stiffer/rigid or uptight position

A professional will use this information as part of their overall **analysis** during an initial consultation, to help build a picture. For example it will help a makeup artist to choose the types of colours and application techniques to use, it will help a hairdresser or barber to identify the types of styles that will suit and work well for the client. It will help a nail technician identify the types of nail, nail colour or nail art that will work best for the client.

Non-verbal communication also includes two other important communication skills, both of which are essential.

1 Listening skills. To find out what the client is saying, for example the types of products they use at home.

2 Reading skills. Reading manufacturer's instructions and client record details and extracting the relevant information is vital to ensure safe working practice.

ACTIVITY

Verbal and non-verbal communication: role play

Practice different methods of communication with a friend. Decide on one of the following topics that you would like to discuss.

- Favourite fashion item

- Favourite film

- Favourite type of food

Try to use different methods of communication during your discussion. Can you identify when your partner is using positive and negative communication?

Physical communication

Physical communication is about being in someone's **personal space**. In the hair and beauty sector you have to physically touch people. This can be very difficult when you first start working with clients.

However, physical communication is an important part of building up *trust* with clients. Clients know by the way they are touched by a person if that person is confident or unsure about what they are doing.

At the beginning of your career in the hair and beauty sector this can be quite frightening or threatening; you may not be used to touching strangers. It is important to learn how to enter a person's personal space without them feeling uncomfortable.

Putting your hand on a clients shoulder or arm when you are talking to them or during a consultation will help break down barriers. This will help the client feel more relaxed so that you can then carry out a treatment or service.

It's a fact!

Personal space is the invisible boundary that surrounds a person's body. That space is required to ensure the person feels and remains comfortable when in the company of others, particularly if they are strangers.

ACTIVITY

Carry out a self-assessment on your communication skills. What are your best communication skills, which ones do you think you need to improve on? Then discuss this with your teacher.

With the support of your teacher develop an action plan to improve on your weakest skills and review your progress at different time intervals.

Understanding how people communicate differently

Not everyone communicates in the same way. Some people use their body language to help express their needs. Others may have a loud voice that booms or vibrates across a room. These characteristics could give you the impression that they are confident people. However, this is not always the case. Sometimes first impressions can be wrong and it is not until you have had time to talk with them that you can form an opinion.

It is part of the role of a good stylist, therapist or technician to identify the best way to communicate with clients so that it builds a good relationship. For some clients this will mean using **visual aids** such as a style book to draw out information to help explain what they want. For others you will need to listen carefully while the client gives detailed information about themselves and what they want.

Bring your learning to life

When you are on your work placement or in a salon environment practice your communication skills with both clients and work colleagues. Keep a daily diary and write down the different communication skills you have used and what effect they had on other people. Discuss your findings with your teacher.

It's a fact! Stereotyping is a way of representing or categorising other people. This may revolve around a certain *characteristic* of a group of people and not looking at them as individuals.

What is discrimination?

The *Oxford English Dictionary* defines the word discrimination as 'the unfair treatment of a person'.

The hair and beauty sector is all about customer care. We are responsible for working closely will all our clients to improve appearance and well-being, we work with all types of people and must not discriminate against any. A professional needs to understand their clients, to ensure that they have identified their requirements and delivered a professional, high-quality service. If they don't their clients may not return and the business may fail, leaving everyone out of work.

Understanding all the different types of communication is very important. We all need to learn more about other cultures and how to communicate effectively with people from different cultural backgrounds. This is no different for the hair and beauty sector where it has become more important to understand different cultures and different communication methods to ensure that a wide variety of people are encouraged to visit our spas and salons to become part of the growth in the business clientele.

What is a stereotype?

The *Oxford English Dictionary* defines the word stereotype as 'a standardised image or idea of a type of person'.

Stereotyping often makes assumptions about people in very narrow terms such as: nationality, disability and sexual orientation. This can often lead to preset ideas or prejudices.

What are prejudices?

A prejudice is a preset opinion or dislike for a person for a specific reason such as race, religion or social group.

Being aware of different cultures and not assuming that everyone is *just like me* will also give you a greater understanding of people and communication skills.

Culture can refer to religion, social, political and family customs. To build a client relationship it is necessary to respect differences. Different cultures have different perceptions on many things. Some cultures use bowing as a form of greeting while others may shake hands, hug or kiss as a method of greeting.

This gesture:

It's a fact!

- In the United Kingdom and United State of America = OK
- In Japan = money
- In Russia = zero
- In Brazil = insult

© Habia

EXTEND YOUR LEARNING

 Many different cultures use different gestures. Can you identify any different gestures and the meanings that they may have in different cultures?

Communication with different client groups

The way you communicate with clients will often be determined by their age, disability, gender and culture.

ACTIVITY

An example of a stereotype could be that all old people are grumpy. Can you think of any others?

It's a fact!

Prejudices can often be formed because of lack of understanding or by influences set by other people.

ACTIVITY

In a group discuss what you understand by the term 'discrimination'. Can you identify different examples of discrimination?

It's a fact!

Did you know that a gesture may have different meanings in different cultures?

If a client is a child it is important to treat them as individuals during the consultation. You will be gathering information not only from their parent or guardian but also from the child.

It is important to:

● Make them feel comfortable and encourage them to talk.

● Make eye contact and if possible talk to them at the same height level.

Some clients may have a disability that needs to be taken into consideration to make sure that you communicate effectively.

For people who are deaf or have a hearing impairment you need to make sure you:

● Have the person's full attention before talking

● Look at the person you are talking to

● Don't mumble, or eat while talking

● Use simple language and short sentences

● Turn down any music or try to avoid background noise

● Use a style book to help gain the right information

● Write down questions or responses if necessary

For people with mobility limitations you will need to:

● Sit at the same level

● Make eye contact

● Treat a wheelchair as the client's personal space

● Talk naturally to the person in the wheelchair, *not* their companion

For people with sight impairments you will need to:

● Touch them on the arm to indicate you are there and are going to talk to them

● Offer them an arm to lead them to the work area

● Make sure you use simple terminology that the client will understand when giving advice

● Remember that the client may not be able to see hand gestures or style books to help explain ideas or to confirm understanding

● Listen carefully to the client and ask questions to make sure you understand exactly what the client wants

● If possible use touch to confirm information

Consulting with clients

The purpose of consulting with client's prior to the service or treatment is to find out exactly what the client's wishes are and if they can be achieved. To do this a professional will need to:

- Examine the client's skin, nails or hair and scalp depending on the service or treatment

- Decide on the most suitable service or treatment and the techniques to use to create the result

- Decide on the most suitable tools and equipment needed to achieve the result

- Decide what products will be needed and advise the client

- Advise the client on the homecare requirements they will need to follow

Top tip

Professional hairdressers make their clients feel at ease by sitting next to their clients during the consultation process, rather than standing over them.

Using open and closed questions

When practicing your consultation technique it is important that all forms of communication are used, firstly to make the client feel welcome and relaxed – especially if they are a new client.

During the consultation it is important that you use a variety of different questions so that you receive the correct information. The use of open questions will help clients give you a better idea of what they want.

Open questions

Open questions can start with any one of the following words:

- Who
- What
- Where
- Would
- When
- How

Any question starting with these words will automatically encourage the client to give you more information than a 'yes' or 'no' response.

Types of **open questions** you can ask your client:

Hair and barbering questions:

- How would you like your hair today?

- When did you last have your hair cut?

- Would you like to change your current hairstyle and if so, what did you have in mind?

- Can you tell me a little bit about your lifestyle?

- What type of job do you have?

- Would you like to look at a style book to help explain what you want?

Beauty and spa questions:

- What is your skin care routine at home?

- What are your main concerns regarding your skin?

- Are you generally in good health?

- Can you tell me if you have any known allergies or sensitive skin?

Nail service questions:

- What is your nail care routine at home?

- Are there any areas that cause you problems?

- Can you tell me if you have any known allergies or sensitive skin?

- How would you like your nails to look, what shape do you prefer?

There are many types of questions you can ask, and once you start asking open questions the response from the client will lead you on to the next question.

Closed questions

Closed questions are used to gain a limited response such as 'yes' or 'no'. They are useful to confirm your understanding.

Types of closed questions you can ask a client:

- Are you having a manicure today?

- Do you usually have your hair parting on the left?

- Do you want me to show you how to apply the products so that you can do it yourself at home?

- Do you want your nails any shorter?

Top tip
Professionals in the hair and beauty sector will always record the details of the consultation process. The records are always safely stored so that they can be used at the next visit.

ACTIVITY

With a friend practice carrying out a consultation service for either a skin treatment, hair or nail service. Don't forget to:

- Speak clearly

- Use open and closed questions

- Vary your voice tone

- Speak with courtesy and confidence

- Use professional vocabulary and not slang

- Never speak while you are eating or chewing gum

- Use positive body language

- Use your listening skills

When you have completed your consultation, write down on a consultation record the information you have gained.

When you have asked clients questions and listened to the response make sure that you confirm the information that you have heard to ensure that both you and the client have understood each other and are clear about the treatment or service agreed before starting.

Finding out what clients want

Clients are vital for the success of a salon business. Without clients there is no business. To make sure that clients always get the best service that the salon can offer salons often carry out research to find out what their clients think about their visit to the salon. They will develop simple client satisfaction questionnaires for the client to complete to make sure that the service the salon is providing is what the client wants.

They will often ask questions such as:

- Did you enjoy your visit?
- What service or treatment did you have?
- Were you looked after at the reception area?
- Were you well looked after by your stylist or therapist?
- Were you offered refreshments?
- Did your stylist or therapist carry out a consultation and give you advice?
- Does the salon offer the right service, treatments or products?
- Do the salon opening times meet your requirements?

 ACTIVITY

Working as part of a team, design a client satisfaction questionnaire.

Think about the types of questions you would like to ask a client to make sure that they keep coming back to the salon.

How would you distribute the questionnaire to clients?

How will you record their answers?

How will you analyse the responses and record the information in a simple report?

What you have learnt

- The importance of creating a good impression:
  - How employers want to create a image for their business
  - How employees reflect the image of the salon
- Professional appearance of the salon:
  - The importance of keeping the salon clean
  - Salon hygiene
  - Cleaning tools and equipment
  - The different sterilisation methods used
  - The importance of following health and safety legislation
- The role of the reception area:
  - The importance of the reception area
  - The skills needed by the receptionist
  - How to answer the telephone and take messages
- Communication and behavioural skills:
  - Understanding and using verbal and non-verbal communication
  - How and when to use physical communication
  - The importance of listening and reading skills
  - Understanding stereotypes, prejudice and discrimination
- Understanding how people communicate differently:
  - Understanding that different cultures communicate differently
  - How to communicate with people of different ages and disabilities
  - How to carry out a client consultation
  - How to use open and closed questions
- Finding out what clients want:
  - Carrying out a client satisfaction survey

Assessment activities

Spot the health and safety problems in the picture below.

Health & Safety in the Salon

List the health and safety issues that you have identified and how you would deal with them.

Crossword

Across

5 Making a decision about something (9)

6 Method of finding out information (7)

8 The terms who, what and why when asking a certain type of question (4)

9 Another term used for health and safety laws (11)

10 The effect you have had on someone (10)

Down

1 Clean and healthy practices (7)

2 A method of verbal communication (11)

3 The name of the person that looks after the reception area (12)

4 A method of sterilising tools (4)

7 A method of non-verbal communication (7)

Wordsearch

```
E M A N U F A C T U R E R W S W O R C
N D I S C R I M I N A T E N M S J S O
E E X O J Q S T N B H C O Z E F S X M
I T C H A A Y Z F R S I E Q J E K S M
G D H N G T Q R S F T V N S G K T O U
Y Y Y O E Z C V P C T L L A M N S T N
H I I Y Z I P E U Z N T S K E U N H I
L H Z E G R R R F F K S K M C J O H C
S Z X S Y U T E M N E I H R N T I O A
X N O I S S E R P M I S A B A N T E T
F S N L N E Y H K X E S S A R E A P I
S Q O I X D K X C R E Y I G A M L Y O
I X I R P I A O F E Y N U D E P U T N
U C T E F C N E G E R G J P P I G O P
E L P T I I R E P Y P U X O P U E E L
M E E S O B W H B N S D T R A Q R R R
Q A C O X R N S G L K N Z S T E H E C
I N E H C A V M A R N G P W E K Q T P
E R R S P B O D Y L A N G U A G E S N
```

Appearance	Disinfect	Messages
Experience	Barbicide	Communication
Clean	Manufacturer	Body language
Impression	Instructions	Stereotype
Reception	Equipment	Discriminate
Hygiene	Regulations	Gesture
Sterilise	Refreshments	

Taking messages

Design a document that can be used in the salon to record messages. The design could include a salon logo.

Make sure that it includes all the relevant information that you need:

- Who the message is for
- Who has taken the message
- The date and time the message was taken
- What the message is
- Any action required
- If the message is urgent
- How to reply to the message (contact telephone number, address, email)

Communication

Can you find pictures from old magazines or from the Internet or draw images that represent different methods of communicating?

- You can display your images on a mood board
- Present your finished display to your class and teacher and explain what each picture represents

3

looking good, feeling great

SANRIZZ Artistic Team

Love of beauty is taste. The creation of beauty is art.

RALPH WALDO EMERSON

Introduction

How you look and behave will form a lasting impression on other people. Think about how you want people to remember you: as fashionable, clean and well-presented? Or do you want people to see you as scruffy and not interested in your own appearance? What impression will this give to employers and to clients in the salon where clients are expecting to be well looked after and that their own appearance be improved?

The hair and beauty sector is about improving a person's image or well-being. An employer wants their employees to represent the business they are working in: they want to create an image that reflects the type of business they are. In the beauty industry an employer may want to reflect a quiet, calm, relaxing atmosphere and this may mean that you will need to wear a simple uniform and no jewellery, whereas in the hair industry, most salons have trendy, fashionable images and your employer may want you to wear fashionable clothes that reflect your own personality as well as the salon's image. However, clothes are not everything. Your personality and how you behave with people will all come together to create that first impression.

What you are going to learn

In this chapter you will learn about:

★ Personal appearance and presentation

★ The expected image and standards required for working in different jobs

★ The expected image and standards expected in the hair and beauty sector

★ How to keep looking and feeling good

Personal appearance and presentation

The way you look, the clothes you wear and the actions you take will send messages to the outside world about how you want people to see you:

● Do you want to stand out from the crowd and be different?

● Do you want to look similar to everyone else and blend into your surroundings?

We all make decisions about how we want to look and the image we show. Some people like to wear outlandish clothes that set them apart from everyone else. They want to be different. Along with the clothes they will also consider the type of accessories, hairstyle or makeup that will complete the look.

iStockphoto.com/gremlin

'Goth' fashion

ACTIVITY

Working in a team, identify different types of clothing styles. For example, think about your friends and other people in your school or college. Think about what they wear, what accessories and makeup they use to complete their image. You may or may not like the clothing other people wear, or the image they have, but this is not important for the purpose of the activity. What is important is that you recognise that different people like to portray different images.

Once you have identified different clothing styles present images for others to see. This could be in a project or by creating a mood board.

It's a fact! Accessories are small additional items of dress such as a belt or jewellery that are used to complete an overall look.

Some people will follow what is currently in fashion and copy styles that they have seen in magazines and shops on the high street. Other people will follow current fashion but give it an individual twist to make it different for them.

© Simon Belcher/Alamy

Current fashion for a female

When you are developing a personal style you need to think about your:

- Height
- Body shape
- Hair style and colour
- Skin tone
- Types and tones of colour

You need to identify styles and colours that suit you and bring out your best features and your personality. It can be helpful to talk to other people such as

© Image Source Pink/Alamy

Current fashion for a male

your friends and family to see what they think suits you. It will help to give you ideas to work from. Some shops also have personal shoppers whose job it is to help you develop a look and style.

EXTEND YOUR LEARNING

 Find out more about the role of a personal shopper and write down what they do.

To make an overall good impression it is not only important to dress right for the occasion. It is about thinking from '*top to toe*', making sure that your overall appearance is good. Your clothes and shoes need to be well looked after, clean and in good repair. Your hair needs to be clean and styled. Your skin should look fresh and clean. If you wear makeup it should be well applied and suit the occasion. Your hands and nails should be well maintained. If you wear nail enamel make sure that it is not worn or chipped. All these little details are needed to complete your total look, create a good impression and send out positive messages.

Positive messages are also given by the way you act and behave. We all act differently with different people. Think about how you act in your different relationships, with your teacher, your parents, with friends or with strangers.

People that work in the hair and beauty sector are working with people all day, some will be regular clients that they have built up a relationship with but many will be new clients that they will be meeting for the first time. We need to make sure we treat all clients in the same professional way. When you are in your training salon or on work experience and have the opportunity to greet a client, remember that you need to look and act professionally.

Think about the following when meeting a client:

- Greet them with a smile - think about them as your friend and then you will naturally start to smile and use open body language

- Don't cross your arms, it can look defensive - make sure that your body is turned towards the person you are talking to

- Make eye contact with the person but be relaxed and don't stare at them when you are talking or listening to what they are saying

- Stand up straight and don't slouch

- Be positive and helpful

Top tip Having good grooming habits and a sense of style is pretty important socially. Unless you have a great personality, people will find it hard to see past a sloppy appearence. Putting thought into your appearence sends out positive messages.

ACTIVITY

Look through magazines or other resources and cut out pictures of the types of clothes and accessories you like to wear. Make a mood board and write a short report covering the following information:

- Why you have chosen the pictures
- The types of accessories you have chosen

Once you have competed your mood board present it to a friend and decide if your chosen pictures fully reflect your style and personality.

The expected image required for different jobs

What you are doing each day:

- Going to school or college
- Going to work

will determine how you will need to adapt your appearance and behaviour. You may have to wear a uniform during the day that restricts the way you like to present yourself. A uniform is often used to identify people to a certain company, organisation or structure, such as the police force, the armed forces and nurses. Not only would you need to wear a uniform but there may also be *restrictions* on how you can wear your hair or if you can wear accessories.

Not all jobs require you to wear a formal structured uniform. Some jobs and careers are more flexible about what you can wear. However, many jobs will create a self-imposed work uniform: think about male office workers or salesmen who tend to wear a suit and tie that conform to an established image.

People who work in shops or department stores also wear a uniform. Sometimes it will be a suit or clothes that identify them as part of the company they are employed by. Sometimes, for example if you are working for Topshop, you may have to wear the clothes that you sell as a way of promoting them to customers.

ACTIVITY

Within a team discuss the good and bad points about wearing a uniform.

ACTIVITY

Identify the images in the first column. Write down in the second column the type of job that these people may have from the uniforms they are wearing.

Types of uniform

Types of jobs people may have from the uniform they are wearing

iStockphoto.com/geotrac

iStockphoto.com//© Uwe Bumann

iStockphoto.com//© Jacob Wackerhausen

© Image Source Black/Alamy

iStockphoto.com/© Christian Nasca

The expected image required within the hair and beauty sector

Most beauty salons and spas will have a formal uniform. They usually want to portray an image of uniformity and harmony within the salon environment, whereas in the hairdressing industry many salons do not have a formal uniform. Some salons will have a colour theme where for example everyone has to wear black. In other hair salons there may be total freedom for employees to wear what they want, enabling you to express your own individual style. However, even if a salon does not have a uniform they may have a salon policy which lays down the rules for what you can and can not wear to work.

Personal appearance and style portrays not only your own personality but also that of the salon image. Even if a person wears a salon uniform they need to take pride in their appearance. A clean and well-presented outfit will give clients confidence. If clothes are dirty and soiled, not only does it give the client a bad impression of that person and the salon but it can also be *embarrassing or upsetting* to clients and colleagues if that person also smells sweaty.

A stylist looking dishevelled and a stylist looking tidy/well-presented

© Habia

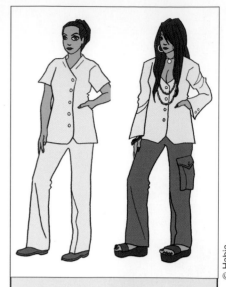

A therapist looking well-presented and a therapist looking dishevelled

© Habia

ACTIVITY

Work on your own or in a group: identify a picture of a salon or spa that you like. Then design an outfit for the employees to wear at the salon or spa. Finally present your finished design.

How to keep looking and feeling good

Personal conduct at work

The way people present themselves and behave at work will show their professionalism. To be a good employee and team member it is important that you get on well with the people you work with. In the hair and beauty sector you are part of a *client-orientated* business. You all have to work together to ensure you give the client a good experience so that they want to return. You have to be *constructive* and *focused* on the job, enjoy what you are doing, and be supportive, open and helpful to other team members.

Many salons will have a work policy that covers personal conduct and this will usually cover aspects such as:

- time schedules for working

- reporting in when absent due to sickness or personal issues

- the dress code

- behaviour

- the salon smoking policy

- the use of drugs and alcohol

- where and when eating and drinking can take place

- health and safety responsibility

- the use of tools and equipment

ACTIVITY

In a team develop a salon policy that covers the salon's dress code:

- The clothes you should wear

- The shoes you should wear

- If jewellery and accessories can be worn

- If and when makeup can be worn

Don't forget to think about health and safety issues and the type of salon or spa that the policy is being developed for.

Always read work policies and procedures. They will provide the information needed to work safely and responsibly.

Preparation is often the key to success at work.

Preparing yourself for work

Becoming a professional within the hair and beauty sector is about preparing yourself so that you are ready for your clients and the treatments and services you will be carrying out. This includes the way you will present yourself to clients, the way to behave and the *discipline* required to work in a *client-orientated business* that *is physically* and *mentally* demanding.

Being prepared for work in the hair and beauty sector is about how you act, the choices and decisions you make and about how you live your life, the food you eat and the way you look after your health. This will all affect how you perform in your work.

- Eating a balanced diet and regular exercise is essential to healthy living, and a sensible attitude to the amount of sleep you need during a working week will enable you to work effectively.

- Understand the effects of drinking alcohol or using drugs will have not only on your body but also on your conduct and behaviour during work.

That is not to say that you should not enjoy yourself. It is about making sure that you can give your best at work and you have the time and energy to enjoy yourself outside of work. It is about getting the right **work–life balance**.

Balanced diet

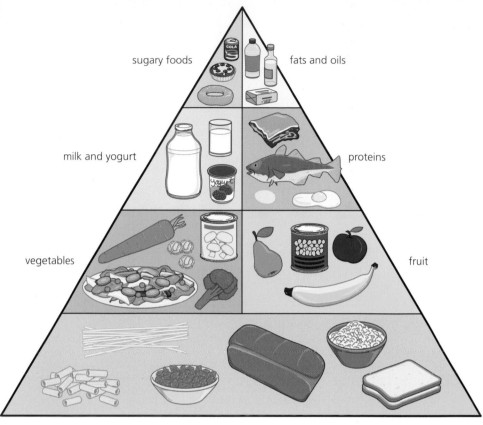

sugary foods

fats and oils

milk and yogurt

proteins

vegetables

fruit

starches

Bring your learning to life

When you are on your work placement or in a salon environment, write a report and include the following information:

- What clothes you have been asked to wear. Do you have to wear a uniform? Does the salon have a policy that you have to follow? Write down the main points from the policy so that you remember them.

- Include in your report how you felt each day. How many hours did you work? What was it like standing on your feet for long periods of time?

- What breaks did you get during the day?

- What jobs were you asked to do?

- How well did you get on with everyone that worked there?

A balanced diet

A balanced diet contains:

FOOD TYPE	WHAT IT DOES	WHICH FOODS YOU CAN FIND THEM IN
Carbohydrates	Give us energy	Found in potatoes, rice, pasta, bread and cereals
Proteins	Enable us to grow and repair our body also give us energy	Found in red and white meat, fish, egg, cheese and milk
Fats	Used as a form of energy *Unsaturated fats* help keep a healthy heart	Found in fish such as tuna and salmon, olive oil and peanut oil
	Saturated fats can raise cholesterol and increase the risk of heart disease	Found in meat, butter, cheese and milk
	Trans fats can raise cholesterol and increase the risk of heart disease	Found in margarine, snack food and fried food
Vitamins	Vitamin A is good for your eyes	Found in meat, vegetables, fruit, fish, nuts, rice, pasta, eggs and butter
	Vitamin B there are different types of this vitamin. They are good for our immune and nervous system and play an important role in cell metabolism	
	Vitamin C helps the body to repair itself	
	Vitamin D is good for the absorption of calcium	
	Vitamin E helps in reproduction	
Mineral salts	*Iron* needed to make haemoglobin in our blood	Found in fish, meat, milk, seeds, nuts, fruit and vegetables and salt
	Sodium used in all our cells especially the nervous system	
	Calcium needed to give us strong healthy teeth, bones and muscles	
Fibre	Used to help the digestive system work properly	Found in fruit, vegetables, nuts, seeds and pulses along with rice and wholemeal or granary bread

Your overall health is reflected in your skin, and if you are feeling under the weather or have been ill for some time then your skin will suffer. The skin needs to have a good blood supply bringing oxygen and nutrients to every cell. Any condition that disrupts this nourishment will have a detrimental effect on the appearance and health of your skin.

It is vital that you eat healthily, drink plenty of water and get regular exercise and fresh air. A healthy balanced diet is essential, containing vitamins such as vitamin C which is said to improve skin healing, and vitamin E which has been used in creams for many years to improve skin condition.

Regular exercise and fresh air is good for your skin.

Many people feel the face can reflect problems in the body. For example, a breakout of spots on the chin could be linked to constipation, or spots under the jaw at either side of the face could be linked to a hormonal imbalance.

EXTEND YOUR LEARNING

You have read about the importance of a balanced diet: now use your research skills to find out about the five a day rule. What does it mean and how will it benefit you?

Personal hygiene

It is vital that stylists, therapists and technicians maintain high standards of personal hygiene. Body hygiene is achieved through daily showering or bathing to remove stale sweat, dirt and any bacteria, all of which create **body odour (BO)**.

Clothes that are restrictive and tight do not allow the air to move around the body and this causes perspiration leading to BO.

- Underwear should be clean and fresh each day.

- Teeth should be cleaned regularly, particularly after eating food. The use of breath fresheners or mouthwash to freshen the breath during the day is a very good idea when working closely with other people.

- *Antiperspirants* or *deodorants* should be applied to the underarms to help reduce **perspiration** and the smell of sweat.

Hands should be washed regularly throughout the day, especially after visiting the toilet and before eating food or carrying out a treatment or service on a client.

- If you wear makeup check that it is still looking good at different intervals during the day and reapply when necessary.

ACTIVITY

Carry out a self-assessment on what your current lifestyle, personal style and appearance is.

- How do you think other people see you?
- What type of impression do you give them?
- Do you eat healthy food?
- Do you exercise?
- Do you have good hygiene habits?

Once you have completed a self-assessment identify both the good and not so good points.

With help from teacher or friend, write a simple action plan of why and how you would like to change or improve some aspects of your current lifestyle, personal style or appearance. Use your action plan to set targets for making changes and review it on a regular basis to see if you have achieved your goal.

How to wash your hands

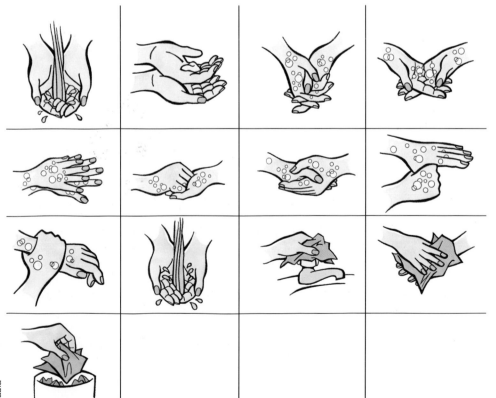

© Habia

Posture

Many of us are concerned with our health. We will reduce the amount of fats, carbohydrates and sugar from our diet and we all have an awareness that exercise is good for you and will tone up muscles but very few of us pay attention to our **posture**.

Making sure that your body posture is correct will help your long term health and to your success in a career in the hair and beauty sector. It will also make you look and feel more confident and give more confidence to your clients. But what is good posture and why is it important? Posture refers the body's **alignment** and positioning with respect to the earths gravity whenever we are standing, sitting or lying down. Good posture enables the force of gravity to be evenly distributed through our body so that no one body part is overstressed.

Like all professionals working in the hair and beauty sector, you will need to learn how to have good posture to ensure that your **stance** is even and that you have good **body balance** as you work around the client. During some treatments and services, particularly in the nail industry, stools or chairs are used so that you work at the correct height and you can maintain your body balance whilst working. However, you need to sit up straight and not slouch. Standing and sitting with the proper *postural alignment* will allow you to work more effectively creating less strain and **fatigue** on your body.

Correct posture

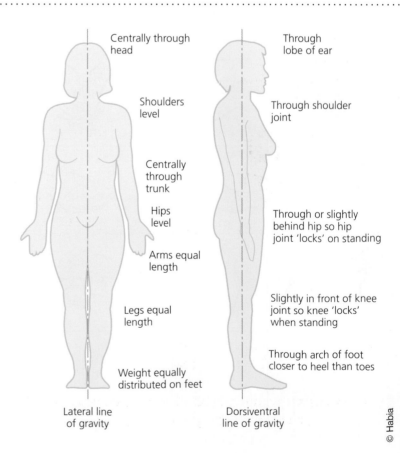

Centrally through head

Shoulders level

Centrally through trunk

Hips level

Arms equal length

Legs equal length

Weight equally distributed on feet

Lateral line of gravity

Through lobe of ear

Through shoulder joint

Through or slightly behind hip so hip joint 'locks' on standing

Slightly in front of knee joint so knee 'locks' when standing

Through arch of foot closer to heel than toes

Dorsiventral line of gravity

© Habia

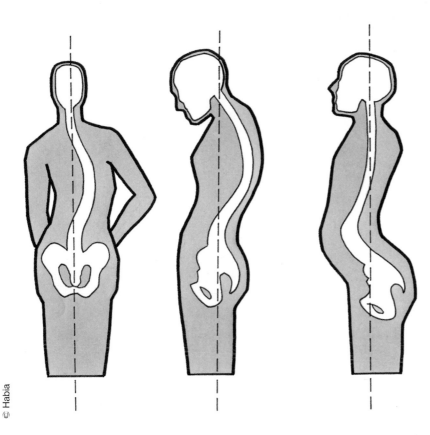

Postural faults

© Habia

Good posture is achieved when your head, shoulders, upper body torso and abdomen, thighs and legs distribute your body's weight evenly over your feet, which should be facing forward and slightly apart. If you move position and lower one of your hips it will change the balance of your body and put more weight on that leg and foot. It will cause the spine to curve and put strain and discomfort on the lower part of your back.

A good way of checking your posture is to stand with the back of your head touching a wall. Your heels should be 150mm from the wall and your bottom touching the wall. Check the distance with your hand between your neck and the wall. If you are within 50 mm at the neck, you have a pretty good posture.

Bad posture is behaviour you learn, you can unlearn it.

It's a fact!

ACTIVITY

Practise standing so that you achieve the correct posture. How does it feel? Is it very different from how you normally stand?

What you have learnt

- Personal appearance and presentation:

  - How the way you look can send out messages to other people

  - How we make decisions about the way we want to look

  - How to make a good impression

- The expected image and standards required for working in different jobs:

  - Why you may need to adapt your appearance

  - Who wears uniforms

- The expected image and standards expected in the hair and beauty sector:

  - The differences between the hair and beauty sector

- How to keep looking and feeling good:

  - How to conduct yourself at work

  - How to prepare yourself for work and the lifestyle choices you make

  - What is a balanced diet?

  - Personal hygiene and how to maintain it

  - The importance of good posture to long-term health and success in the hair and beauty sector

Assessment activities

Crossword

Across

1 A type of accessory (4)

3 A person's individual characteristic (11)

5 You wear it as part of a job (7)

6 The way you look (10)

8 Sending out a good signal (8)

9 Another term for behaviour (7)

Down

1 Stale sweat and dirt create this (4, 5)

2 Keeps you healthy (8)

4 The effect you create on someone (10)

7 The way you stand (7)

Wordsearch

```
J P E R S O N A L I T Y M L S W N
B Y Q U B F N G F D Z G R G A P W
A Y O O R M P P M H V T O I R O D
M C I I G S E W D N V E F P F S V
P I W V D V E V A R F I I R A T I
R L X A T A F H G C V D N O C U T
O O D H D P T F T M N H U T C R A
F P E E A P H G W O F O N E E E M
E W E B D E L O I D L J E I S U I
S G P C F A C H U V G C T N S W N
S G I M N R S Q V O C C F S O K S
I M A G E A A Q O I U E T D R W D
O N A P F N L H K D V Y H A I C V
N X R C U C J A N R L L G X E Z T
A N I T P E W O B E K R S B S X H
L K N R O S C I M P R E S S I O N
P E R S P I R A T I O N K L N L H
```

Posture	Personal	Diet
Impression	Behaviour	Clothes
Appearance	Uniform	Policy
Accessories	Personality	Conduct
Fashion	Perspiration	Balance
Image	Vitamins	Professional
Style	Protein	

Foods and food groups

Identify the type of food in the left-hand column and write down in the right-hand column the food group or groups that it supplies.

TYPE OF FOOD	FOOD GROUP

iStockphoto.com/ZoneCreative

iStockphoto.com/© Gene Krebs

iStockphoto.com/shapecharge

4
get ahead in hair styling

Sharon Cox @ SANRIZZ

Fashion is something that goes in one year and out the other.

UNKNOWN

Introduction

Have you ever looked at photographs of your parents, carers or relatives and laughed at the way they used to wear their hair? Of course, at the time the photograph was taken, the hairstyle was probably very trendy, but as the fashions for clothing changes, so does the fashion for hairstyles.

Hair is probably one of the first things you notice about another person, but it is not all about fashion.

Certain hairstyles can be a clue to your personality, cultural background or even your religion.

Hairstyling is a fun thing to do. You can easily and temporarily change your appearance, and if you don't like the new look you can wash your hair and start again.

You may find that you have a creative flair for styling your own hair. If you do, you could if you want to, use this talent to learn the skills of a professional hairdresser or barber, and one day, look after the hair of others.

In this chapter you will learn about all about hair, how to look after your own hair and the techniques for creating some hairstyles.

What you will learn

In this chapter you will learn about:

★ Hair and hair structure

★ The factors you must consider before styling hair

★ The differences in hair types

★ How your personality, the occasion, gender and culture can influence the way hair is styled

★ Why you must be aware of health and safety when styling hair

★ How to shampoo and condition the hair and scalp

★ How to style hair

★ How to use styling tools, products and equipment

★ The way history influences how hair is styled

Hair structure

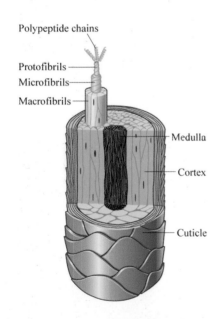

Polypeptide chains

Protofibrils
Microfibrils
Macrofibrils

Medulla

Cortex

Cuticle

Hair – what is it?

Before you can begin to look after, care for or style your hair, you need to know what hair is.

Hair structure

Hair is made up of three sections:

- Cuticle

- Cortex

- Medulla

Cuticle

The cuticle is the outer section of the hair. It is made up of overlapping layers of **translucent** scales. When magnified, the scales look a little bit like tree bark, in the way that each layer lies over the other.

If the cuticle is in poor condition, the cuticle scales will be uneven or broken.

It's a fact! A smooth cuticle makes it easier to brush and comb the hair and reflects the light to give a glossy appearance.

It's a fact! Hair in poor condition will tangle easily because the cuticle does not lay flat and smooth. Light will not be reflected and the hair will look dull.

Bring your learning to life

You can find out if the cuticle of your hair is in good condition by carrying out a **porosity test**. This test is carried out on the hair before it is shampooed. You need to take a small bundle of hairs, holding the ends of the bundle together with one hand. Using the thumb and forefinger of the other hand you gently stroke the hair from the ends to the roots to feel the condition of the cuticle. If the hair feels smooth it means that the cuticle is laying flat and that the hair is in good condition. However, if the hair feels rough and tangles together when testing, it is an indication that the cuticle has been damaged and that the hair is in poor condition.

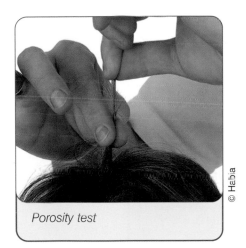

© Habia

Porosity test

Dr John Gray

Cortex of hair

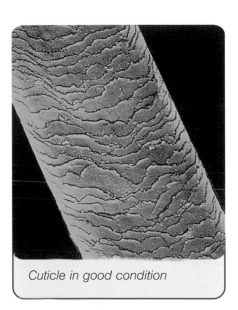

Cuticle in good condition

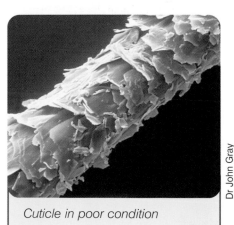

Dr John Gray

Cuticle in poor condition

Cortex

The cortex is made up of layers of long, intertwining, cigar-shaped cells. The structure of these cells gives the hair its strength and elasticity. If the cortex is in good condition, the hair will stretch and return to its normal length. This means that you will be able to change the amount of curl you have in your hair – you will be able to make your hair curly or straight. If the cortex is in poor condition, the hair will be damaged and will easily break when stretched into a new position.

Melanin is found inside the cortex. Melanin is the natural colour of hair. You can see the colour of your hair through the translucent layers of the cuticle.

Medulla

Not every hair has a medulla. Coarse hair is more likely to have a medulla than fine hair. The medulla is made up of soft spongy cells with air spaces.

When hair is wet it stretches more than when it is dry.

It's a fact!

The hair in the skin

The hair grows from the hair bulb through a special opening in the skin. The skin is made up of several layers, and you can learn about the layers of the skin in Chapter 5, Face Facts.

Cross-section of hair and appendages

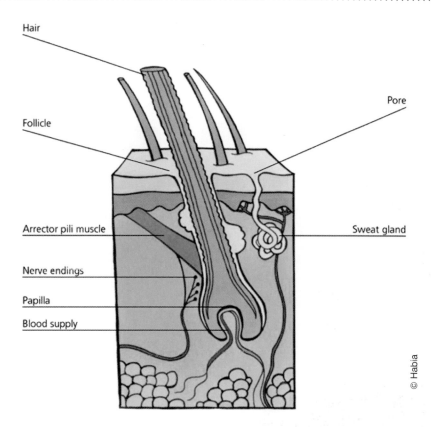

Hair

Follicle

Pore

Arrector pili muscle

Nerve endings

Papilla

Blood supply

Sweat gland

© Habia

Follicle

The follicle is a tube in the **dermis** that holds the hair in place. The size of the follicle varies and the follicles for the *terminal* hair on your head will be larger than the follicle for *vellus* hair.

Sebaceous gland

This is the gland that produces the natural oil of the hair and scalp called **sebum**.

Sweat gland

The sweat gland produces a substance called **sweat** which, when it evaporates, is used to cool the skin when you get hot.

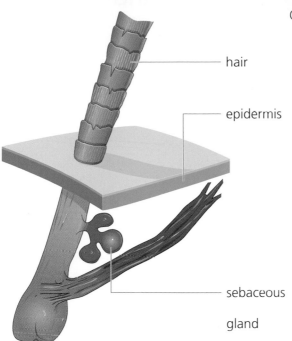

Close-up of the sebaceous gland

hair

epidermis

sebaceous

gland

If you are cold, the raised hair will help to trap warm air. You can clearly see the actions of the arrector pill muscle on your arms.

Close-up of the sweat gland

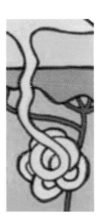

Arrector pili muscle

If you get cold or frightened this muscle will contract, making 'goose pimples' on the skin and raising the hair. Sometimes, if the hair is short enough, it will stand on end.

Papilla

This is the point at which all new cells for hair growth are produced. When first formed, the cells produced are very soft, but they are hardened and shaped as they are forced into the follicle and out onto the surface of the skin.

Nerve endings

The hair does not have its own nervous system, so you cannot feel when the hair shaft has been cut. The follicle is surrounded by nerves which enables you to feel any movement in the hair.

Blood supply

The blood supply to the hair is very important, as it carries nutrients that ensure healthy hair growth. The blood supply enters the papilla through a series of fine small blood **capillaries**.

Close-up of the arrector pili muscle

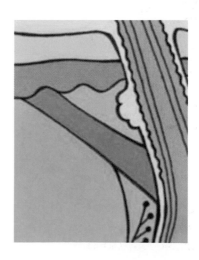

Close-up of the papilla

Factors affecting hair care and styling

If you want to achieve a good hairstyling result, you must consider the following factors before you begin.

1 The shape of the head

2 The shape of the face

3 The shape of the body

4 Lifestyle

5 The direction of hair growth

6 The amount of natural curl in the hair - hair type

7 The texture of hair

8 The strength or elasticity of hair

9 The amount or density of hair

10 The length of hair

11 Any skin, hair or scalp conditions that may affect hair care and styling

The shape of the head

The bones of the head form the head shape.

It's a fact! The bones of the head are known as the **cranium**. The cranium is made up of eight bones.

The size of certain bones in the cranium makes a variety of head shapes. In particular, the bones that make the biggest differences to the head shape are the **frontal bone** – which is the forehead, and the **occipital bone**, which is found at the back of the head. The shape of the **parietal bones** produces differences in the shape at the top of the head.

Professional hairdressers are very good at ensuring the shape of the head is well balanced when they are styling hair. For example, if you have a very large forehead, they would tell you that a wearing a fringe would suit you. If you have a very narrow forehead, they will tell you *not* to wear a heavy, full fringe.

The cranium

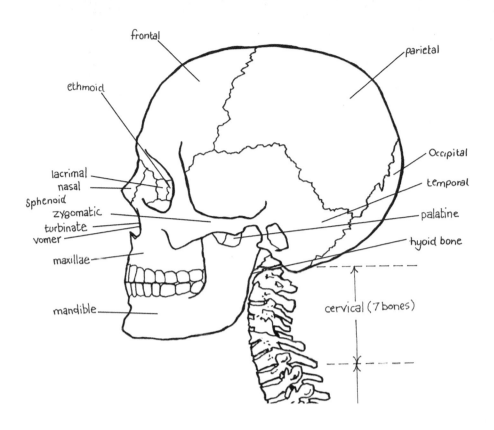

Head shapes

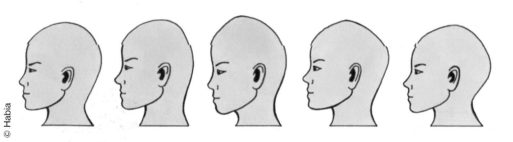

© Habia

EXTEND YOUR LEARNING

Look in some hairstyling magazines and find examples of hairstyles that would suit people with high foreheads, narrow foreheads, pointed heads and heads that are flat at the back.

ACTIVITY

Look at the different head shapes of people in your class. You are more likely to see the shape of the head on people with short hair.

Bones of the face

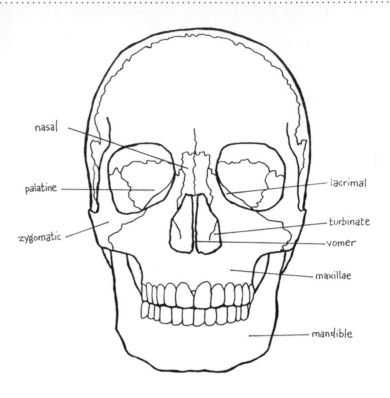

The shape of the face

Facial shapes can be:

- Oval
- Round
- Square

- Rectangular
- Long
- Heart or triangular

- Pear
- Diamond

Shapes of the face

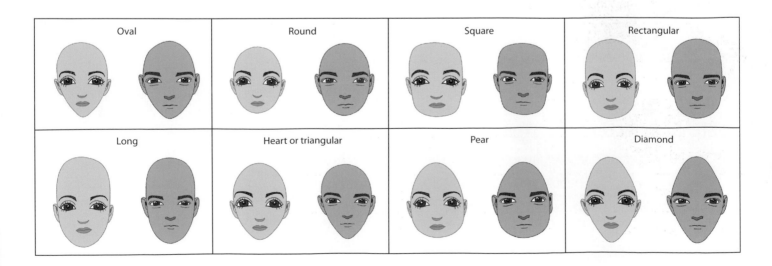

To find the shape of your face you have to look at:

- Length of your face from the top of your forehead to the tip of your chin

- The width across your face from ear to ear

- The shape of your jawline – this can be curved or angular

- The height and shape of your forehead

- The shape of your chin

ACTIVITY

Take all the hair away from your face, then work with a partner (or look in a mirror), and identify the shape of your face.

	Tick
Length of the face	
The length of my face is *much* longer than the width	
The length of my face is the *same* as the width	
The length of my face is *a little* longer than the width	
Jawline	
The shape of my jawline is *angular*	
The shape of my jawline is *curved*	
The width of my jawline is *wider* than my forehead	
The width of my jawline is *narrower* than my forehead	
Chin	
The shape of my chin is *pointed*	
The shape of my chin is *curved*	
Forehead	
My forehead is *high*	
My forehead is *narrow*	

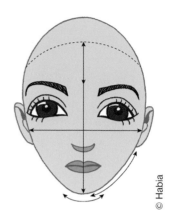

Guidelines for analysis of your facial shape

© Habia

As a rough guide, look at the diagrams of the facial shapes again. You can also read the statements below and to help you decide the shape of your own face.

- An **oval** face is a little longer than it is wide, wider at the forehead than at the chin, with a *curved* jawline and chin

- A **round** face is the same width and length, with a *curved* jawline

- A **square** face is the same width and length, with an *angular* jawline

- A **rectangular** face is much longer than it is wide with an *angular* jawline

- A **long** face is much longer than it is wide with a *curved* jawline

- A **heart**-or **triangular-shaped** face is a little longer than it is wide, wider at the forehead than at the chin, with a curved jawline and a pointed chin

- A **pear-shaped** face is a little longer than it is wide, narrower at the forehead than at the chin, with an angular jawline

- A **diamond-shaped** face is much longer than it is wide with a narrow forehead and pointed chin

---

EXTEND YOUR LEARNING

 Look in magazines and find an example of the different facial shapes.

Stick all the different facial shapes on one page and label them.

The shape of the body

Everyone has a different body shape – even if you are an identical twin, one twin could weigh more or less than the other.

- Some people are tall and slim with long arms and legs

- Some people have wide shoulders and a narrow waist

- Some people have a rounded shape with short arms and legs

The shape of the body must be considered when styling hair. For example, if you are very tall and very slim, a professional hairdresser would *not* recommend a hairstyle that is also tall and thin as this would not be flattering. However, if you are short a hairstyle with height can make you look taller.

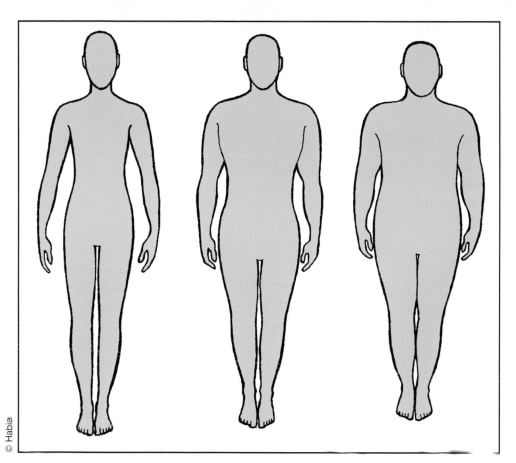

Body shapes

EXTEND YOUR LEARNING

 Look in magazines of hairstyle magazines and find pictures of people with different body shapes. Stick all the different body shapes on one page and label them.

Areas for different hair growth patterns

Lifestyle

Are you a busy person? Do you have lots of things to do after school or college? How much spare time do you have? These are all questions that a professional hairdresser will ask you when you request a new hairstyle. You have to be sure that you will have the time to look after it.

The direction of hair growth

Do you have a fringe where the hair will just not lay flat – it sticks up in one particular place? Or, if your hair is short, do you find that the hair at the nape of

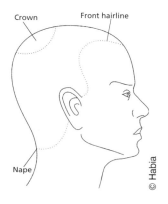

Crown
Front hairline
Nape

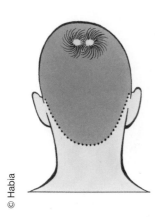

Double crown

© Habia

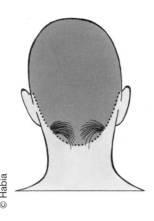

Nape hair growth patterns

© Habia

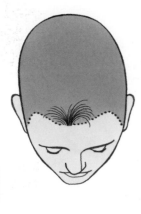

Cowlick

© Habia

your neck will not lie evenly? If you have said yes to these questions, then you have something known as an **adverse hair growth pattern**.

Your hair grows in different patterns all over your head. There are three main areas where you can see the different patterns: the crown, the nape and the front hairline.

Hair growth patterns at the crown

The **crown** is the area at the top of the head. At this point you can see the circular growth pattern of the hair. Most people only have one crown, but some have a **double crown**. If there is a double crown, you will be able to see two separate areas of circular growth.

It's a fact! Sometimes the 'crown' or circular area of hair growth is not at the top of the head but is found on the side of the head, or lower down towards the back of the head.

Hair growth patterns at the nape

These swirling patterns of hair at the nape of the neck are known as **nape whorls**. For example, the hair may grow from the left side of the nape to the right, sometimes, the hair can grow in opposite directions. If the hair grows in opposite directions towards the centre, it forms a tail of hair at the centre of the nape.

Hair growth patterns at the front hairline

The two most common patterns of hair growth at the front hair line are known as a **cowlick** and a **widow's peak**.

Cowlick

A cowlick is usually found on one or both sides of the hairline at the forehead.

Widow's peak

A widow's peak forms a point at the centre of the forehead hairline. Sometimes the hair grows back from a deep point at the centre of the forehead, or the hair on both sides of the centre of the forehead can grow into the middle to form a point.

Hair growth cycle

Does your hair grow quickly? Or have you tried to grow your hair long, and found that it never seems to grow past your shoulders? The speed in which hair grows varies from one person to another.

Bring your learning to life

Work with a partner and record your hair growth patterns by ticking the appropriate box. You should look for the following:

Front hairline

Do you have:

- Cowlick? ☐
- Widow's peak? ☐
- A front hairline *without* an adverse hair growth pattern? ☐

Crown

Do you have:

- A single crown? ☐
- A double crown? ☐

Nape

In which direction do your nape whorls grow?

- Hair that grows from the right side to the left ☐
- Hair that grows from the left side to the right ☐
- Hair that grows away from the centre towards the front ☐
- Hair that grows into the centre ☐
- A nape hairline *without* an adverse hair growth pattern ☐

Widow's peak

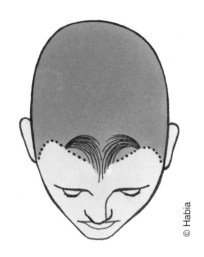

© Habia

It's a fact! The hair on our head grows, falls out and grows again in a continual cycle of time that can last anything from 1,5–7 years and grows at an average rate of 1.25 cms each month

Each stage of hair growth has a special name. The names that describe the different stages of hair growth are:

- Anagen
- Catagen
- Telogen

It's a fact! The papilla is found in the hair bulb

Anagen

Hair is continually growing in this stage of hair growth. For some people this stage will only last for 1.5 years – for others, this stage will last for up to 7 years.

Top tip A useful website is http:// guinnessworldrecords. com/records/human_body

EXTEND YOUR LEARNING

Look on the Internet or read the *Guinness Book of World Records* to find images of a person who has the longest hair in the world.

http:/guinnessworldrecords.com/records/human_body

It's a fact! The follicle is created before birth.

If the follicle did not rejoin the papilla a new hair would not grow. You see this on some males and the condition is known as male pattern baldness. Sometimes the hair does not re-grow because of a condition known as **alopecia**.

A useful website is http://www.keratin.com/ ac/baldnesspatterns/ baldnessclassification

Hair growth cycle

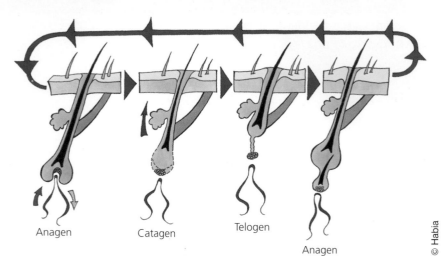

Anagen Catagen Telogen Anagen

© Habia

EXTEND YOUR LEARNING

Investigate the appearance of different types of alopecia

Alopecia can affect any area of the body where there is hair.

The hair can grow during the anagen stage because it is receiving nourishment from the blood supply at the **papilla**.

Catagen

This is a very short stage of the hair growth cycle: it only lasts for around two weeks. During this stage the **follicle** rests and new hair growth stops.

Telogen

This stage is the complete resting stage of hair growth and lasts for about four months. The follicle then rejoins itself to the papilla and blood supply and a new anagen stage begins.

Male pattern hair loss

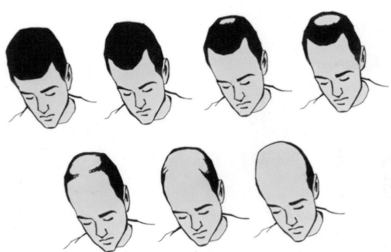

© Habia

EXTEND YOUR LEARNING

Investigate the patterns for male pattern baldness

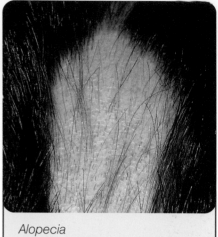

Alopecia

The amount of natural curl in hair-hair type

Some hair is curly, some is straight and some is wavy. The amount of natural curl in the hair is known as hair type.

Hair can be classified into three generic types:

- African

- Caucasian or European

- Asian

African-type hair

African type hair is generally very curly, and often frizzy, but the type of curl can vary from soft, open curls to tight, woolly hair. This hair type is generally dark in colour – often brown, dark brown or black, but can also be red or blonde. The hair is very crinkled, it grows in a variety of directions before it appears to gain length.

This type of hair is not only found on people of African descent, but can also be found on people of *mixed race*. Sometimes, hair with similar characteristics to African-type hair – tight, frizzy curls – can be seen on a person with white skin and of European descent.

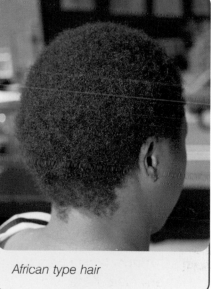

African type hair

Hairstyle created on African-type hair

Hairstyle created on African-type hair

Cross section of African type hair

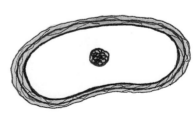

Top tip Treat African-type hair very gently when brushing and combing to prevent damage and breakage.

It's a fact! African-type hair may look coarse, but it is often very fine and delicate, meaning that the hair is likely to break before reaching a great length.

It's a fact! If you look at African-type hair under the microscope you will see that the cross-section of the hair is almost kidney-shaped.

Cross section of Caucasian type hair

© Habia

Caucasian or European-type hair

The look of Caucasian or European hair can vary a great deal. This type of hair can be straight, wavy or curly, coarse or fine in texture. The colours range from black to the palest blonde. The reason for the differences in British hair is because people from all over Europe and beyond have invaded and lived in the British Isles for hundreds of years.

It's a fact! If you look at Caucasian hair under the microscope you will see that the cross-section of the hair is oval in shape.

It's a fact! Caucasian hair is never the same from one person to another. It can be coarse and curly or fine and straight, it can have the characteristics of African-type hair or those associated with Asian hair.

iStockphoto.com/© Miodrag Gajic

Blonde, straight hair is linked to the Viking people who invaded Britain in 878AD

iStockphoto.com/© Famke Backx

Red hair can be linked to the Celts from Scotland

Colin Anderson/Brand X/Corbis

Dark brown glossy hair can be linked to the Romans who ruled in Britain from 43AD

Asian-type hair

Asian hair can be the dark glossy hair that you associate with India or Pakistan, or it can be the much straighter Oriental-type hair that can be found in China and Japan. Asian hair is normally very dark brown or black in colour.

It's a fact!

Asian hair grows much faster than that of Caucasian or African-type hair. Asian hair is often much coarser than the Caucasian or African type.

It's a fact!

If you look at Asian hair under the microscope you will see that the cross-section of the hair is round.

Asian hair

Dr John Gray

Hairstyle created on Asian type hair

Hair by Reds Hair and Beauty, Sunderland. Photography by John Rawson @ TRP.

Hairstyle created on Asian type hair

Hair by Reds Hair and Beauty, Sunderland. Photography by John Rawson @ TRP.

Hairstyle created on Asian hair

Hair by MK. Photography by Andy Lynch - www.andylynch.org

The texture of hair

Hair texture is measured by the *diameter* of a single strand of hair. The larger the diameter, the coarser the hair is.

Coarse hair

Coarse hair can sometimes feel quite dry. People with coarse hair normally have less hair per square centimetre than those with fine hair.

Medium hair

Medium hair falls between the diameter of coarse and fine hair.

Cross-section of Asian hair

© Habia

Coarse hair can have up to 11 layers of cuticle

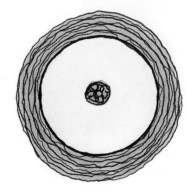

© Habia

Medium hair may have around seven layers of cuticle

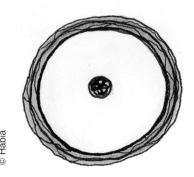

© Habia

Fine hair may only have four layers of cuticle

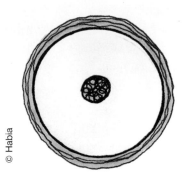

© Habia

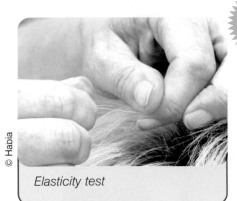

© Habia

Elasticity test

It's a fact! An average head of hair has 100,000 individual strands. People with fine hair can have as many as 150,000. People with coarse hair may only have 80,000.

Fine hair

Fine hair may only have four layers of cuticle. Because of this, the hair may be more likely to be damaged.

The strength or elasticity of hair

Hair that is in good condition is able to stretch and return to its original length. The amount of elasticity in the hair depends on the condition of the **cortex**. If your hair is damaged and the elasticity is reduced you will not be able to style it as easily as hair that is in good condition. You can check the amount of elasticity in your hair by carrying out an **elasticity test**.

The amount or density of hair

Hair density is the amount of hair that is present on the head. *Sparse* means that there is not much hair. *Abundant* means there is lots of hair. If you can see the scalp through the hair, the hair is sparse.

The length of hair

The length of hair is critical when styling hair. If the hair is too long or too short for the chosen hairstyle, it cannot be created.

ACTIVITY

Compare the diameter of one of your hairs to that of your friends. Who has the coarsest hair in your group, and who has the finest?

It's a fact! It is possible to have very sparse, coarse hair and very abundant, fine hair and vice versa.

Bring your learning to life

Work with a partner to carry out an elasticity test. Hold a single strand of hair and support it at the roots to ensure comfort. Gently stretch the hair, and then release it observing how soon it returns to its natural position. Hair that is in good condition will stretch and then immediately return to its normal position. If the hair has reduced elasticity, the hair may return to its natural position more slowly. However, hair that is very poor condition may stretch and not return or may break under the slightest pressure.

Skin, hair and scalp conditions that may affect hair care and styling

There are many hair and scalp diseases and disorders that can affect hairstyling. Some conditions are not infectious. However, if an infectious or contagious condition exists, then the services must not be carried out.

CONDITION	CAUSE AND SYMPTOMS	TREATMENT
Bacterial condition Folliculitis 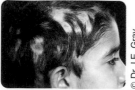 © Mediscan	Bacteria enter the opening of the follicle causing an infection. The opening of the follicle can become inflamed and painful **Note** Can be spread by direct and indirect contact with a person, by dirty tools and towels or by irritation from chemicals	• Refer for medical advice • Hair services must not be carried out
Fungal condition Ringworm of the scalp © Dr J.E. Gray	Patches of pink skin surrounded by a red ring. The centre of the patch is covered in grey scales of dead keratin and if on the scalp the hair will break leaving stubble	• Refer for medical advice • Hair services must not be carried out

Ringworm is not caused by a worm.

It's a fact!

It's a fact! A parasite is an animal or plant that lives on a host, which can be another animal or plant. The parasite gets its nourishment from the host.

Parasitic condition
Head lice

© iStockphoto.com/ arlindo71

Small parasites that live on the scalp and feed by sucking blood. The lice lay eggs called **nits**

Head lice are passed from one person to another by head-to-head contact

- Refer for pharmacy advice
- Hair services must not be carried out

Hair and scalp disorders

CONDITION	CAUSE AND SYMPTOMS	TREATMENT
Split ends Cr J.E. Gray	Damage to the hair shaft of longer hair which causes the ends of the hair to split. Sometimes the split hair occurs on the length of the hair shaft	• Cut them off! • Prevent split ends by keeping the hair in good condition and have regular haircuts to keep the split ends at bay • Hair services can take place
Dandruff © Mediscan	Dry scalp leading to shedding of excess, white skin flakes, caused by underactive sebaceous glands	• Special shampoos formulated for the treatment of dandruff • Hair services can take place **Note** If the dandruff is yellow or smells, then medical treatment may be required and hair services should not take place
Very dry hair	Caused by overuse of chemicals, electrical equipment or exposure to extremes in weather conditions, such as sunlight. Another cause can be underactive sebaceous glands	• Special shampoos formulated for the treatment of dry hair • Regular applications of conditioner and deep conditioning treatments • Hair services can take place
Very oily hair and scalp	Caused by an overactive sebaceous glands. Sometimes related to changes in hormones, such as during puberty	• Special shampoos formulated for the treatment of oily hair and scalps • Hair services can take place

EXTEND YOUR LEARNING

There are many other parasites that live on humans. Investigate what they are. Warning! Some are quite gruesome. There are even some that live in the eyelashes of *most* people...but don't worry – they are harmless.

> **Top tip**
>
> Put the word *Demodex folliculorum* into a search engine and see what you find!

Bring your learning to life

Now you are aware of all the factors that affect hairstyling, look in a hairstyle magazine and choose at least three different hairstyles that you would like to wear.

The hairstyles should be for:

- An everyday hairstyle. This hairstyle should be one that you will be allowed to wear for school or college. The hairstyle should be suitable for your cultural and racial beliefs.

- A special occasion hairstyle. This hairstyle could be for a festival, celebration or party.

- A hairstyle for the future. This hairstyle should be one you cannot achieve now, but would want to achieve in the future. Your hair may be too long or too short to achieve the hair at the moment.

Cut out the pictures and stick them on three separate pieces of paper or card. On the paper or card note down the results of the factors for hairstyling you have to consider about yourself.

Make a note of the following:

- The shape of your head
- The shape of your face
- The shape of your body
- Your lifestyle
- The direction of your hair growth
- The amount of natural curl in your hair - your hair type
- The texture of your hair
- The strength, or elasticity of your hair
- The amount, or density of your hair
- The length of your hair
- Any skin, hair or scalp conditions you may have that may affect hair care and styling

The everyday hairstyle

Make a plan about how you will achieve your everyday hairstyle. On the paper or card for your everyday hairstyle, list the products, tools and equipment you will need to achieve the result you would like.

Style your own hair, or have it styled for you in your chosen everyday hairstyle.

Take a photograph of the final result and add the image to your paper or card.

The special occasion hairstyle

Make a plan about how you will achieve your special occasion hairstyle. On the paper or card for your special occasion hairstyle, list the products, tools and equipment you will need to achieve the result you would like.

Style your own hair, or have it styled for you in your chosen special occasion hairstyle.

Take a photograph of the final result and add the image to your paper or card.

Hairstyle for the future

Make a plan about how you will achieve your hairstyle for the future. On the paper or card for your future hairstyle, make a note of the changes you will need to make to your hair to achieve the look you would like.

Influences on hairstyling

When you decide to style your hair what influences you most? Is it your friends, movie stars, people in bands, in magazines or those you see on the television?

Hair and history

When a hairstyle or make-up trend is worn by a celebrity, promoted on television or shown in the latest magazines, you might think that something new has been created, but the hairstyles you see today have been developed over many years and can be traced back to another time, place, culture or civilisation.

Ancient Egypt to the present day

Follow the timeline for a classic hairstyle known as a *bob*. See how the hairstyle of today still has some of the influences from thousands of years ago in another land and culture.

ANCIENT EGYPT	1920s	1960s	TODAY

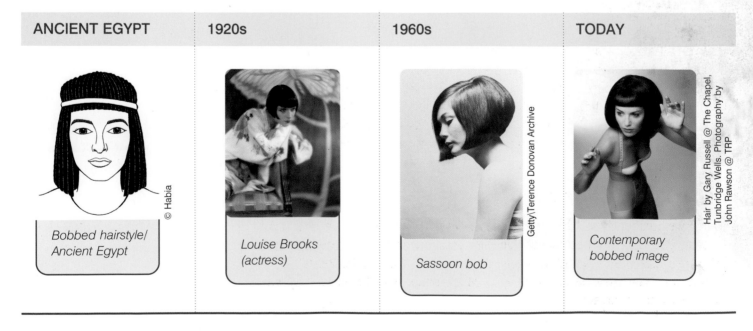

Bobbed hairstyle/ Ancient Egypt

© Habia

Louise Brooks (actress)

Sassoon bob

Getty\Terence Donovan Archive

Contemporary bobbed image

Hair by Gary Russell @ The Chapel, Tunbridge Wells. Photography by John Rawson @ TRP

Ancient Greece to the present day

This simple but elegant long hairstyle is influenced by a character in Greek mythology known as Psyche.

ANCIENT GREECE	VICTORIAN	TODAY

Psyche, Goddess of the Soul

Victorian version of the psyche knot

Long hair styled with influences of the psyche knot

John William Waterhouse

From Girls Own Paper and Woman's magazine, 1911

© iStockphoto.com

Hair and different occasions

Hairstyles are also influenced by the occasion that you are going to wear them for. For example, hair may be worn very simply for work or school, but may be styled to look different when attending a wedding, your school prom or another special occasion.

ACTIVITY

On an A4-sized card, make up a collage. Begin with a photograph of yourself in the centre of the card wearing your everyday hairstyle. Then, arranged around your photograph, add hairstyles that would be suitable for your own culture, hair length, type and texture that you could wear for different occasions. For example, a hairstyle that you would wear to a friend's party, one that you would wear as a guest at a wedding or for your prom.

Hair and personality

Your own personality will also determine how you style your hair. If you are *extrovert* you may want to reflect this with your hairstyle. With your hair you can make statements about yourself. You can say 'I am outrageous'. Alternatively, you may be *introverted*, in which case, your hairstyle may say, 'I am shy and reserved'.

ACTIVITY

Find a range of images which could represent your own personality and stick them on a page. Then find other hairstyles that may suit people of different personalities. Add these to your page and state which personalities the hairstyles may represent.

Hair and culture

The word *culture* has many meanings, one of which is the importance of activities that people take part in. For example, the activities you take part in may mean that you like to keep your hair covered. It is part of your culture to do so. It is what you believe is right for you and it is something that all the members of your family do.

For other people, styling and showing off their hair is what makes them happy. They believe that their hair can reflect their lifestyle and their identity – who they are.

In black culture the natural appearance of hair is seen as a way of representing the history and background of the people of African descent.

West Africa to the UK

The braids and plaits worn today, known as corn rows, are influenced by the traditional hairstyling techniques of West Africa.

WEST AFRICA	TODAY
 *West African hairstyle, plaited*	 *Plaited hair*

Wikipedia Commons: Roaveig Thattai

© Habia

An Afro hairstyle

© iStockphoto.com/Izabela Habur

African-type hair can also be used to celebrate the culture of being black. One hairstyle that is used for this is the '**Afro**'. For this hairstyle, instead of flattening and straightening the hair, the natural characteristics are used and it is dried by blow-drying the hair out from the head. This type of hairstyle was worn with pride and showed the world that Black is Beautiful.

Hair and gender

Who do you think cares more about how their hair looks – men or women? If you look back in history you will see that men's hairstyling has been at least as elaborate as women's, if not more so.

	MEN		WOMEN	
Medieval	Wikipedia Commons	A man with a medieval hairstyle	Wikipedia Commons	A woman with a medieval hairstyle
Elizabethan	iStockphoto.com/Vincent Voigt	The short hairstyle of Elizabethan man	iStockphoto.com/Duncan Walker	Simple straight hair with centre parting worn in Elizabethan times
1700s	Wikipedia Commons	A man in an elaborate wig	Wikipedia Commons	A woman in an elaborate wig
1800s	iStockphoto.com/Chepatchet	Victorian men's hairstyle – elaborate moustache	iStockphoto.com/Duncan Walker	Simple women's Victorian hairstyle – centre parting, neat

EARLY 1900s

Wikipedia Commons

Edwardian men's hairstyle showing stylised moustache

Wikipedia Commons

Simple Edwardian women's hairstyle

LATE 1900s

Popper foto/Getty Images

1960s Mod boy

Getty/Popper foto

1960s Mod girl

TODAY

Lee Moran @ SANRIZZ

2000+ men's hairstyle

Scott Smurthwaite @ CREAM

2000+ female hairstylc

ACTIVITY

Carry out a survey with the boys and men, girls and women you know that have an interest in styling their hair. Design a questionnaire to find out who spends the most time and money on the appearance of their hair. Discover which types of products are used by each sex.

Give the questionnaire to an equal amount of boys/girls/men/women so that you can easily compare the results.

You can look at the results of boys against girls and men against women. Or you can look at the results of girls and women against boys and men.

When you have completed your survey, create graphs to illustrate the results.

Find out the results from the survey and state who spends the most time and the most money on the appearance of their hair. State which hairstyling products are used by both sexes, and those products that are only used by either males or females.

Top tip

It is important to only do the survey with people that have an interest in styling their hair, or you will not be comparing like with like.

Shampooing and conditioning the hair and scalp

If you want to have a hairstyle that looks good, the starting point has to be hair that is clean and in good condition.

The health and safety of shampooing and conditioning hair

Having wet hands and using certain products can lead to the development of a condition known as **contact dermatitis**, which, if protection is not used, can be contracted by people who work in the hair and beauty industries.

This is an itchy skin condition caused by an allergic reaction to the products or materials. The symptoms of contact dermatitis are:

- Red and dry hands
- Itching
- Flaking skin
- Swelling on the hands
- Blistering

After services such as shampooing hair you must wash and carefully dry your hands. Then apply a good hand cream to protect them. Wearing disposable and

It's a fact!

Up to 50% of the 180,000 hairdressers will suffer from work related dermatitis at some time in their career. So – look after your hands!

Top tip Habia have produced a guide on dermatitis and glove use for hairdressers. An online version is available on **http://www.habia.org/uploads/Dermatitis%20Booklet.pdf**

non-latex gloves will protect the hands from water and chemicals help to prevent contact dermatitis.

Shampoo and conditioning products

How do you choose your shampoo and conditioning products? Do you look at the colour of the products to see if it matches the bathroom? Do you buy a product because you like the shape of the bottle?

There are so many products available it can be confusing, but if you look carefully, you will see that the products are categorised so you can choose one that is suitable for you. There will be products for different hair and scalp conditions, for different hair types and hair textures.

Before you choose a product, you should know:

- The hair type
- The hair texture
- The condition of your hair and scalp

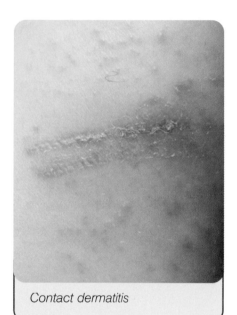

Contact dermatitis

ACTIVITY

Analyse your own hair and scalp by completing the following analysis questionnaire. When you have done this, try it out again by asking another person the same questions

Frequency of shampooing

(a) I have to shampoo my hair every day

(b) I have to shampoo my hair every 3–5 days

(c) I only need to shampoo my hair once each week

Appearance of hair

(a) My hair looks lifeless if I do not shampoo it every day

(b) My hair is shiny

(c) My hair looks dull

Appearance of the scalp

(a) I have sticky scales on my scalp

(b) I have no scales on my scalp

(c) I have flaky skin on my scalp

Answers

Mainly (a) you have oily hair

Mainly (b) you have normal hair

Mainly (c) you have dry hair

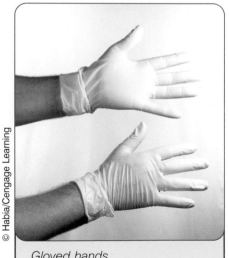

Gloved hands

Shampoos and conditioning products for different hair types

Hair *type* refers to the amount of curl in the hair. Some shampoos and conditioners are designed for use on very curly or frizzy hair. These shampoos will have special ingredients which smooth and coat the cuticle layer to make the hair easier to comb. They will also make the hair shine. Shampoos and conditioners for very straight hair are designed to highlight the glossy appearance that is possible to achieve with flat, straight hair.

Shampoos and conditioning products for different hair textures

Hair *texture* refers to the diameter of a single strand of hair. Very fine hair can be made to look and feel thicker by the special ingredients in some shampoos and conditioners. The ingredients will coat the hair shaft and make the hair feel thicker. Shampoos for very coarse hair will have extra conditioning ingredients to make the coarse hair feel silkier.

Shampoos and conditioning products for different hair and scalp conditions

You need to know if your hair is dry, oily or normal, and, if your scalp is dry, oily or dandruff-affected before you can choose a suitable shampoo or conditioner.

Conditioners

There are two different types of conditioner:

- **Surface conditioner**
- **Penetrating conditioner**

Surface conditioner
Surface conditioners work by coating the outside layer of the hair known as the cuticle and are applied after the shampoo. Once you have dried your hair, the cuticle scales lay flat and your hair will look shinier.

Penetrating conditioner
You can use a penetrating conditioner if your hair is in very poor condition. Sometimes hair is naturally very dry because the **sebaceous glands** that produce the natural oil, sebum, are under-productive. Or perhaps the hair may have been damaged.

Hair can be damaged by:

- Chemical damage such as perming, relaxing, chemical straightening, colouring and bleaching

Top tip **You can apply heat** yourself by covering the hair with something that will retain the body heat from your head. A good way to do this is by using a plastic shower cap.

- Physical damage, such as overuse of heated styling equipment such as straighteners or thermal irons

- Environmental damage, such as over-exposure to the wind and sun

A penetrating conditioner is applied to hair that has been shampooed, and then heat is applied. The added heat opens the cuticle layer, allowing the conditioner to enter the hair shaft. Professional hairdressers and barbers use a variety of electrical equipment to add heat during a conditioning treatment.

It's a fact! **Some conditioners** are designed to be applied and are not rinsed from the hair. These are known as **leave in-conditioners**.

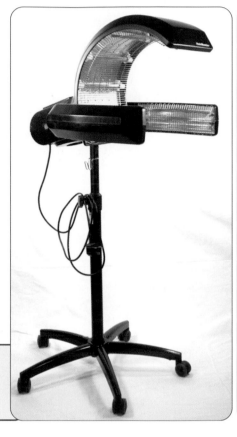

© Habia

Steamers and accelerators are used to open the cuticle during a penetrating conditioning treatment

Courtesy of KeraCare

Shampoo and conditioning products for African-type hair by Avlon

The electrical equipment used for penetrating conditioners includes:

- steamer

- accelerator

- infrared heater

Shampooing products

All product manufacturers will make a range of shampoo and conditioning products for different hair types.

EXTEND YOUR LEARNING

Investigate the full range of shampooing and conditioning products by looking on the manufacturer's websites. Useful inks are **http://www.clynol.com**; **http://www.loréal.co.uk**; **http://www2.wella.co.uk** and **http://www.avlon.com**

Shampoo and conditioning products by L'Oréal

Bring your learning to life

When you are in a salon on work experience or in your training salon you will be able to use some professional shampoo and conditioning products. When you have used them, complete the table below.

PRODUCT	WHY I LIKED THIS PRODUCT	RESULTS
Write the manufacturers name and the brand name of the product that you used in this column	State why you liked the product – for example, did you like the smell, how it felt, how it was packaged, how it looked?	Write down the results achieved from using the product. For example, did the products leave the hair in good condition; perhaps the shampoo lathered well or left the hair tangle-free? Perhaps the product was easy to rinse from the hair.

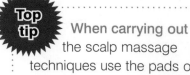

Top tip When carrying out the scalp massage techniques use the pads of your fingers and not the tips. Ensure that your nails are not too long.

Scalp massage used for shampooing and conditioning

There are different massage movements and, if you are shampooing the hair of another person, you must use the correct movements to ensure that the massage is comfortable.

MASSAGE	USED FOR	MASSAGE MOVEMENT	PURPOSE
Effleurage © Habia	Shampooing and conditioning	Smooth, flowing, stroking action	• Spreads the shampooing and conditioning products • Cleanses the length of long hair during the shampoo process. The stroking movement ensures that the long hair does not tangle • Ensures that conditioner is spread to the lengths and ends of long hair
Rotary © Habia	Shampooing	Rotating, round, revolving, circular action	• Cleanses the hair and scalp
Friction © Habia	Shampooing	Fast, short rubbing action	• Stimulate the blood supply on the scalp. This causes the scalp to tingle and feel clean • Increase the blood flow to the muscle of the scalp, which covers the cranium
Petrissage © Habia	Conditioning	Rotating, round, revolving, circular action	• Stimulate the blood supply on the scalp. An increased blood supply will provide the nutrients to the new hair cells that are developing in the **papilla**. • To increase the production of sebum from the sebaceous glands • To relax the client

Step by step methods for shampooing hair

Shampooing hair

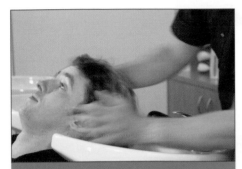

1 The client is gowned for a shampoo and the head is positioned for client comfort and to ensure a watertight seal at the basin.

2 Protective gloves are worn and the temperature of the water is tested to ensure client comfort. The hair is evenly wet prior to the application of the shampoo. Note how the hand is cupped near the ear to prevent water running onto the client's face.

3 Shampoo is poured into the palm of the hand prior to applying to the scalp.

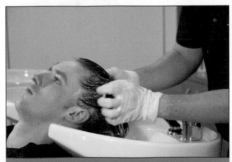

4 *Effleurage* is used to spread the shampoo evenly through the hair and then the scalp is cleansed using *rotary* and *friction* techniques. The hair is shampooed twice.

5 Shampoo is rinsed from the hair ensuring the scalp and hair are free from product.

6 A towel is wrapped around the head at the end of the shampoo treatment.

Step by step methods for conditioning hair

Conditioning the hair with a penetrating conditioner

1 The conditioning product is placed into a small bowl.

2 The product is applied to the hair using a tinting brush.

3 An *effleurage* massage technique is used to spread the conditioning product evenly through the lengths of the hair.

4 The hair is lifted to ensure the fingertips can touch the scalp. The massage is carried out using *petrissage*.

5 To retain the body heat a plastic head cap is placed over the scalp. A hair dryer is used to add additional heat. The additional heat will allow the cuticle scales to lift and the product to enter under the cuticle scales. At the end of the treatment, the conditioner is rinsed from the hair ensuring the product is removed from the scalp and hair.

Conditioning the hair using a leave-in conditioner

1 Following the shampoo, leave-in conditioner is applied to the hair.

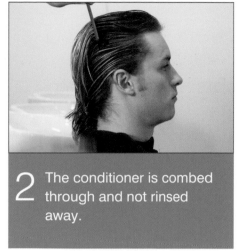

2 The conditioner is combed through and not rinsed away.

Bring your learning to life

When you are in the training salon or in your work placement, work with a partner to shampoo and condition each other's hair. When you do this for the first time, you should ask your partner for feedback about the pressure you are using for the massage techniques. Check that the pressure is comfortable and relaxing.

When you have finished the service, write down your experiences in your Diploma file. Have a photograph taken of yourself when carrying out the shampoo service. How professional do you look?

Tools and equipment for hairstyling

There is a wide range of tools and equipment that you can use for styling hair. Some are available for personal use.

Health and safety

When you style hair, you must ensure that:

- You work carefully and safely
- Your tools and equipment are sterilised and are suitable for the work you are doing

When you are applying products for shampooing, conditioning, styling and finishing, you need to ensure that:

- You read the manufacturer's instructions.
- Check that the products you are using are suitable for the type of hair they are to be used on.
- The application of the product does not lead to damage of hair, skin or clothes.

Tools

The tools you need to carry out hair styling will vary according to the hairstyle you wish to create.

Combs

You will need a variety of combs to carry out combing techniques on different *types* and *textures* of hair. The combs should be made from materials that prevent damage to the hair structure.

Your own combs should be kept clean with hot soapy water and only used for one person. Professional combs must be sterilised between uses.

Top tip

Avoid the use of hairbrushes that are made from damaging man-made materials or have hard bristles.

	USE	BENEFIT	TIP
Wide-tooth combs	For combing hair to remove tangles for styling	The wide teeth are good for coarse, dense hair, or very curly hair	Always comb hair from the points to the roots to prevent damage
Wide and narrow tooth combs	For combing a variety of hair types and textures	The wide teeth are good for coarse, dense hair, or very curly hair. The fine teeth are good for combing very short hair and backcombing	Do not use the fine teeth on coarse, curly or frizzy hair
Tail combs	For making sections when setting and styling hair	The tail of the comb enables you to make clean, neat sections. This means that you will be able to work methodically and efficiently when styling and dressing hair	Use the point of the tail to make the sections
Afro pick	For use on very tight, curly or frizzy hair	The wide teeth enable the combing of this hair type	Comb from the outside edges of the hair, into the centre

Hairbrushes

Professional hairdressers and barbers need a variety of hairbrushes that are suitable for different hair *types* and *textures*.

Your own hairbrushes should be kept clean with hot soapy water and only used for one person. Professional hairbrushes must be sterilised between uses.

	USE	BENEFIT	TIP
Flat-back brushes	For brushing hair during drying and styling	Removes sectioning marks after setting. Prepares hair for styling. Removes tangles from hair	Do not use brushes on wet hair as this would cause the hair to stretch
Paddle brushes	For brushing hair during drying and styling	Removes sectioning marks after setting. Prepares hair for styling. Removes tangles from hair. Massages the scalp	The cushioned base and gentle bristles means this type of hair brush is good for massaging and stimulating the scalp of dry hair. Do not over-use on hair that is naturally oily, as stimulating the scalp will produce more sebum
Radial brushes	For creating curls in hair when blow drying, or for smoothing and straightening curly hair	Lifts the hair at the roots to create volume	Use a small radial brush to create tighter curls and a large radial brush for large curls
Vent brushes	For styling during blow drying	The open back of the brush allows the air to pass through to quicken the drying time	Use on straight hair to create texture

Equipment

If you want to create a wide range of hairstyles, you will need a variety of setting and styling equipment.

All equipment should be made from materials that will not damage the hair.

Your own equipment should be kept clean with hot soapy water and only used for one person. Professional equipment must be sterilised between uses.

	USE	BENEFIT	TIP
Velcro™ rollers	For creating soft curls and movement in hair	Soft, natural-looking curls. Adds volume to hair	Only use Velcro™ rollers on dry hair. The small teeth on the rollers attach themselves to the hair shaft and will not work on wet hair
Rollers	For creating curls and movement in hair	Different-sized curls can be produced using different-sized rollers	Use large rollers to create big, open curls and small ones for tight curls
Pincurl clips	For making pincurls in hair	Curls the hair without lifting from the roots	Use small sections when creating the pin curl
Hair bands, pins and grips	For holding long hair in place	Keeps a long hairstyle neatly in place	Use dark-coloured pins on dark hair and pale-coloured pins on light hair to help to disguise them
Diffuser	Attached to a hand-held dryer	Dries hair without disturbing natural curl	Use the dryer speed on a low setting to prevent 'frizzing' curly hair

© Habia and Cengage Learning

Afro pick attachment	Attached to a hand-held dryer	Straightens hair as it dries	Keep the dryer on a medium heat to prevent burning the scalp and damaging the hair
Back mirror	To enable the client to see the back of the hairstyle	Ensures the client is happy with the finished result	Hold the mirror to one side so the image is reflected back into the main mirror
Sectioning clips	To clip hair into sections	Enables you to work in a logical and methodical way	When inserting the sectioning clips, open them fully to prevent pulling the hair
Trolley	To store tools and equipment	Keeps tools and equipment safe and tidy	So you don't have to bend over to reach the trolley, keep it on your right-hand side if you are right-handed and vice versa. This will prevent back strain and injury

Electrical equipment

Hair can be dried, curled, straightened, pressed and crimped with specialised equipment. Professional electrical equipment is designed for all-day-long use.

Electrical equipment should be used following the manufacturer's instructions and for the purpose for which it is intended. Check equipment before you use it. Look at the plug and ensure there are no loose or exposed wires. Check the cable for fraying or damage. Professional electrical equipment must be checked for safety once each year by a qualified person.

	USE	BENEFIT	TIP
Hand-held hair dryer	For drying, and styling hair	Portable and easy to use	Use the different adjustable temperatures and speeds to suit your hair texture and density. Fine hair will need a cooler, slower setting than dense, coarse hair
Straighteners	For straightening and curling hair	Can be used to create a variety of effects	Use moisturising products to protect the hair from heat damage
Tongs	For curling hair	Can be used to create a variety of different sized curls	Use small barrel tongs to create tight curls and large barrel tongs for soft curls
Pressing comb	For smoothing very curly and frizzy hair	Can be used to smooth and blend unevenly relaxed hair	Use on the hairline to straighten where straighteners cannot reach
Crimpers	For creating a zigzag or waved appearance to hair	Can be used to create a variety of looks	Crimp longer, one length hair for the best effects
Thermal irons	For smooth curls and movement in the hair	Can be used to create a variety curl sizes – even on very short hair. Heated in an oven	Use thermal irons to straighten the regrowth of chemically straightened hair

Heated rollers	For creating waves, curl and movement	Can be used on long and short hair to produce a quick result	Only use on dry hair
Hood dryer	For drying hair	The whole head can be dried at the same time	Check the temperature to ensure client comfort
Steamer	For creating moist heat	Steam opens the cuticle to allow conditioners and some chemicals to enter the cuticle	Only use distilled water to prevent limescale
Accelerator	To create dry heat	Can be used to dry hair and to speed up the process of chemical treatments	Place the equipment to ensure even distribution of heat over the whole head

Products for styling hair

When styling hair you need to use different products to protect, strengthen, reduce or create curl, add moisture to dry hair or shine to dull, dry hair.

Different types of styling and finishing products

All product manufacturers will make a range of styling and finishing products for different hair types. Many products can be used in combination with each other to help you provide the result you want to achieve for the total look.

Courtesy of Namaste

Styling and finishing products for African type hair by Namaste

ACTIVITY

Investigate a product range of styling and finishing products. Identify the products that are best used to provide:

- Styling support
- Added moisture to hair
- Added strength to hair
- Added shine to the hair
- Protection against the environment, for example, from the sun or from swimming
- Heat protection, for example, from heated styling equipment

Write down the names of the products. If you can find images of the products, use them to illustrate the product range.

Courtesy of L'Oréal

Styling and finishing products for men by L'Oréal

It's a fact! Finger drying means that hair is dried using the fingers to create the movement instead of styling equipment.

It's a fact! A roller with a small diameter will produce a tighter curl than a roller with a large diameter.

Styling hair

Changing your hairstyle can change your whole appearance.

To create hairstyles you can make hair look curly or wavy or you can make hair look straight and smooth. You can also finger dry hair.

Step by step methods for making hair curly and wavy

Creating curls and waves by setting hair in rollers

This technique is used to create longer lasting curls, waves, volume and movement.

1 Styling product is applied to wet hair.

2 Sections of hair are taken to match the width and the depth of the roller to be used.

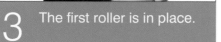

3 The first roller is in place.

4 Rollers are placed in a brick formation.

5 The roller set is complete.

6 The hair is dried under a hood dryer.

7 The finished result.

It's a fact!

If lift and volume is required, hair is set *on base*.

© Habia

If you want to decrease the amount of volume in the hairstyle; you position the rollers *off base*.

© Habia

Creating curls and waves by blow drying

A radial brush can be used to create curls, waves, body and movement in hair.

1 Styling product is applied to the hair.

2 The hair is sectioned and a radial brush is used to create curl and movement.

Top tip

To avoid burning the client, keep the air from the dryer pointed away from the scalp.

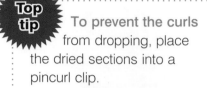
Top tip To prevent the curls from dropping, place the dried sections into a pincurl clip.

3 The sides of the hair are wound into the radial brush and dried with the hair dryer.

4 The finished result.

Creating curls and waves by setting hair on heated rollers

1 Heated rollers are placed into the hair in a brick formation.

2 Finished result.

© Habia

Other methods for creating curls and waves in hair

1 Curling tongs of different sizes will create different-sized curls.

2 Curls can be created by turning straighteners as they are moved down the hair shaft.

3 Tight waves can be created by using crimpers.

4 The natural curl in hair can be increased by using a diffuser attachment on a hand-held hair dryer.

5 Velcro rollers can be used to create soft curls, wave and volume.

Bring your learning to life

Work in a pair or use a mannequin head block to create curls or waves. Take a photograph of the end result and record the results in your Diploma file. Identify what you did well and what you would do better next time.

Step by step methods for making hair straight

With heated electrical equipment and the improvement in products to maintain the condition of hair, it is possible to temporarily straighten most hair types.

Making hair straight by using a wrapping technique

The wrapping technique is used to smooth hair and uses the shape of the head to create movement.

> **Top tip**
>
> The prolonged use of straighteners is not recommended as this can lead to hair damage and breakage.

1 The client before styling.

2 A styling product is applied and a large roller is wound into a section at the crown area.

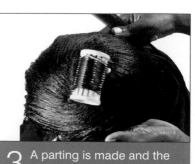

3 A parting is made and the wrap is started by combing and directing away from the parting. At the same time, the other hand is used to smooth and blend the hair around the roller.

4 The finished wrap.

5 A net is applied to the wrap and the client is placed under the hood hair dryer.

6 The finished result.

It's a fact! The position of the roller at the crown is known as the '*point of origin*'.

Making hair straight by blow drying (radial brush)

By using a large diameter radial brush, hair can be smoothed and straightened.

1 The client before styling.

2 The hair is sectioned and gently stretched by placing the radial brush on top of the hair.

3 The process is repeated at the sides of the head.

4 The process is completed at the front of the head. Note how smooth and straight the hair is.

5 To create texture and movement the client tips their head back and cool air is blown into the hair from the dryer.

6 The finished result.

Making hair straight by blow drying and electrical equipment (paddle brush and straighteners)

1 The client before styling.

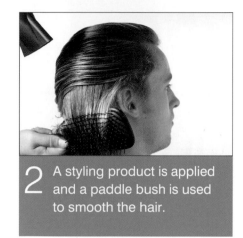

2 A styling product is applied and a paddle bush is used to smooth the hair.

3 A heat-protective product is applied and straighteners are used to smooth straighten the hair.

4 Finished result.

Making hair straight by using a rake attachment and thermal tongs

Top tip

Practice opening and closing the barrel of the tongs and rotating the tongs.

1 The client before styling.

2 A rake attachment is used with a hand-held dryer. The rake is combed slowly through the hair, working from the ends to the roots.

Top tip As pressing combs get very hot, you must check the temperature before applying it to the hair. To test, place the heated pressing comb on tissue. If the tissue becomes scorched, or burns, the comb is too hot and must be cooled by placing on a prepared cooling pad. The cooling pad is a pre-dampened, folded towel.

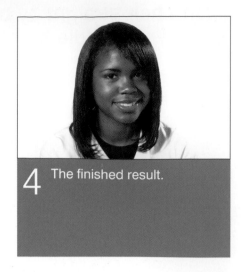

3 When dry, the hair is re-sectioned and thermal tongs are used to smooth and straighten the hair.

4 The finished result.

Other methods for making hair straight

1 Hair can be smoothed using a flat back brush.

2 Hair can be straightened using a pressing comb.

Bring your learning to life

Work in a pair or on a mannequin head block and use techniques to straighten and smooth hair. Take a photograph of the end result and record the results in your Diploma file. Identify what you did well and what you would do better next time.

Step by step methods for finger drying hair

Finger drying is styling the hair using a hand-held hair dryer and your fingers. It is a very quick technique, but it only works well on short layered hair.

© Habia and Cengage Learning

Technological developments

Hairstyling today is much easier than it was even a decade ago, and certainly easier than a century ago. This is because of the technological developments in tools and equipment. For example, combs and hairdryers have improved dramatically over the last two centuries. (Combs, made out of tourmaline and carbon today, were made out of bone in the 17th century and horn in the 18th century.)

EXTEND YOUR LEARNING

 Choose a product, tool or equipment used for styling hair and research its history. Make a timeline.

What you have learnt

- About hair, what it is made from, the different types of hair and where hair grows on the body

- Factors including head and face shape hair type and texture, hair density, hair growth:

  - The factors include head and face shape hair type and texture, hair density, hair growth patterns

- How to take account of the differences in hair types:

  - There are three generic hair types: African, Asian and Caucasian

  - Mixed race hair is a mixture of the different generic hair types

  - Hairstyles should be chosen to suit the characteristics of the hair type

- The diverse hairstyles that can be created:

  - Hair can be made curly or wavy, or hair can be straightened to produce a range of different hair styles

- How to use products, tools and equipment for haircare and styling:

  - Always read the manufacturer's instructions before using and applying products

  - Check electrical equipment before use

- How to style your own hair and that of others:

  - Carry out a consultation to ensure that the hairstyle chosen is suitable

  - Style hair using the correct products, tools and equipment for the intended hairstyle

- The key historic hair trends that influence the hairstyles you wear today:

  - Hairstyles worn today are influenced by those worn over many centuries in different civilisations

  - Culture, identity and religion may determine the way hair is worn

- The technological advances which aid haircare and styling:

  - The tools, products and equipment we use today ensure safer and easier hairstyling

- The terminology related to haircare and styling

Assessment activities

Crossword

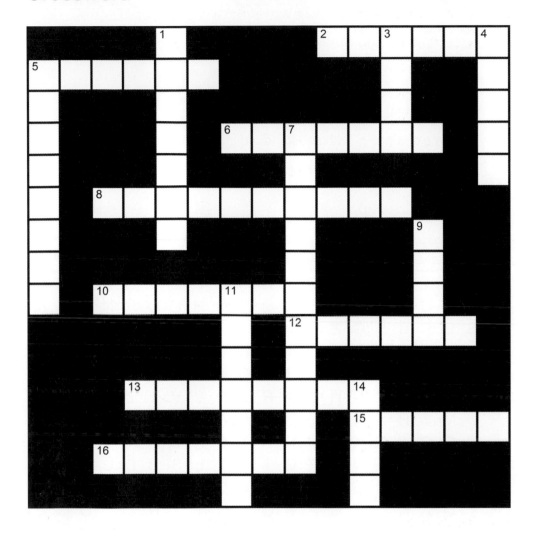

Across

2 Wear these to prevent dermatitis (6)

5 This is used to make curls in hair (6)

6 Not all hairs have one of these (7)

8 Another name for a heart shaped face (10)

10 The outer layer of hair (7)

12 The main section of the hair (6)

13 This comb is used for making neat sections in hair (4, 4)

15 A hair type that is usually very straight and dark (5)

16 A type of hair that is very tightly curled (7)

Down

1 Hair is made from this (7)

3 This facial shape is similar to the shape of an egg (4)

4 This is the natural oil of the hair and skin (5)

5 A fungal infection of the scalp (8)

7 The name that is given to more than one crown (6, 5)

9 A hair texture (4)

11 The name of a hair growth pattern found at the front hairline (3, 4)

14 The place on the head where the occipital bone is found (4)

Wordsearch

```
C M M T N G N J G P W H J F L L S Z K F N
A L L U D E M A I G P N N H L O R N O T N
H S U R B D G Z C M C D O A C U N C I I O
C I X N U P I A T I P B V C E A E G P P I
S H A M P O O I N G R O J S C G Q O C U T
C A T A G E N H C A R F P V V I Z J F N C
R U M S R E N E T H G I A R T S P I I A I
L Q O R I G X P H R R T C R O W N I V I R
T E L O G E N X F G I V T L S B D U T S F
R E C T A N G U L A R A G W R O U N D A J
N Y D A N D R U F F O V N Y J R L C O C L
E G A R U E L F F E G G I G R E O Z C U P
L E U Y I G F O S P P Q N B U L U G H A I
R G L Y T G I G P E R S O N A L I T Y C C
O X R C C I N Z S M V N I S Z O A A K U R
H E E O I O S I D D E R T K E R S R L I A
W D C T W T M O L S M X I N H B Q T A H N
O R X I R T U B R Y H C D Q V A U H X M I
V Z J E L O H C S O T I N S E R A M M O U
E L A S T I C I T Y P S O P E S R Q Z W M
P E T R I S S A G E D D C U Z S E Z C G B
```

African	Crown	Long	Round
Anagen	Culture	Medulla	Sebum
Asian	Cuticle	Occipital	Shampooing
Bones	Dandruff	Oval	Square
Brush	Effleurage	Personality	Straighteners
Catagen	Elasticity	Petrissage	Styling
Caucasian	Friction	Pins	Telogen
Comb	Grips	Porosity	Triangular
Conditioning	Growth	Rectangular	Whorl
Cortex	Hair	Roller	
Cranium	Lice	Rotary	

Match the statements

Hair grows and then falls out in a continuous cycle. Match the statements to the correct stage of the hair growth cycle by drawing an arrow from one to the other.

Anagen	This is a very short stage of the hair growth cycle. It only lasts for around two weeks. During this stage the follicle rests and new hair growth stops.
Catagen	This stage is the complete resting stage of hair growth. During this time, the follicle completely separates from the papilla for around four months
Telogen	Hair is continually growing in this stage of hair growth. For some people this stage will only last for 1.5 years – for others, this stage will last for up to 7 years.

Colour in the bones

Colour in the frontal, parietal and occipital bones

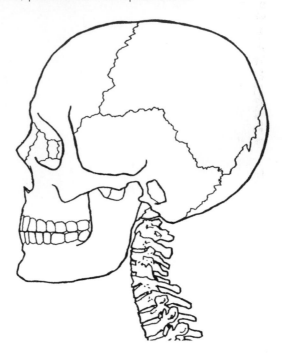

True or False

Read the statements – are they true or false?

	TRUE	FALSE
Terminal hair is soft and downy and found on the faces of women		
Hair in good condition will have a smooth cuticle		
A porosity test is used to find out the condition of the cuticle		
All hairs have a medulla		
Sebum is the natural oil of the hair		
A cowlick is found at the nape of the neck		
Head lice are a parasite		
The hair has a muscle called the arrector pili		
African-type hair is straight		
Hair texture is the diameter of a single strand of hair		

5
face facts

Love of beauty is taste. The creation of beauty is art.

RALPH WALDO EMERSON

Leonardo Rizzo @ SANRIZZ

Introduction

The world of beauty therapy and skin care can be a very exciting place. You can make someone feel and look better from just one visit to the salon. Beauty therapy is a world full of different treatments and skin care is just one small but important aspect of what beauty therapy is all about. You will learn about some of the ranges of skin care products available for you to use, but before you use them you will need to learn about the skin, its structure and characteristics.

In this chapter you will learn about the skills and knowledge needed to understand how to look after your skin. Your skin will reflect how you feel, what you eat and how healthy you are. Looking after your skin is important when you want to look and feel at your best. You will learn how to carry out a simple skin care routine that you can use every day but also how to carry out that routine on other people.

What you are going to learn

In this chapter you will learn about:

★   The perceptions of facial beauty

★   Skin structure and skin conditions

★   Preparation needed for carrying out skin care routines

★   Skin care routines and treatments

The perceptions of facial beauty

How beauty is influenced by our culture

Everyone thinks about facial beauty in a different way. What one person sees as beautiful may not be beautiful to another. How beauty is perceived, what facial features are considered beautiful or how we enhance our appearance will vary from one person and culture to another. In addition, the use of skin products may or may not be totally acceptable or tolerated by some cultures – they may even be discouraged.

Certain cultures may frown upon the use of skin care products, because it is seen as too superficial and frivolous and encourages vanity. In other cultures, mothers pass skin care secrets and techniques down to their children, so that they develop good skin hygiene and try to avoid teenage blemishes.

 ACTIVITY

Have you ever thought about where your own views of beauty have come from? Is it from your family and friends, watching celebrities on the television or in films, or from magazines that tell us who looks good and who doesn't?

In a group discuss what you think is meant by the term facially beautiful. Can you agree on what or who is or isn't beautiful?

How beauty is influenced by our culture

The structure and function of the skin

The construction of skin is a fascinating subject. The skin is our largest organ yet we often take it for granted. The skin varies in appearance according to race, sex and age. Our skin will change from season to season and will reflect general health, lifestyle and diet.

During **puberty** our hormones become more active, causing the skin to become oily which often creates blemishes and spots on the skin's surface. During our twenties the skin is at its best as the hormone imbalance should now be stable. As we move into our thirties fine lines start to appear on the skin surface particularly around the eyes. At forty our hormone activity becomes less active and the skin starts to lose its strength and elasticity. The skin becomes drier and small lines and wrinkles appear on the surface of the skin. In our fifties small brown patches start to appear on the temple area of the face and the back of the hands. All this is part of life and it is up to us to care and protect our skin from damage such as ultraviolet light from the sun.

The skin is made up of two main layers: the epidermis which provides waterproofing and serves as a barrier to infection, and the lower layer called the dermis, which is home for the **appendages** of the skin.

How beauty is influenced by our culture

The epidermis

The epidermis is the outer layer of the skin: the one that you can see and touch.

The main function of the epidermis is to protect the deeper living structures within the dermis.

- The main type of cell found in the epidermis is the **keratinocyte**, which produces the protein **keratin**.

- Keratin makes the skin tough and reduces the passage of substances in and out of the body.

As cells move closer to the surface of the epidermis they mature and then die and are constantly rubbed away or naturally shed.

There are five layers of the epidermis, and each one has different characteristics.

The five layers are:

- Horny layer (stratum corneum)

- Lucid layer (stratum lucidum)

- Granular layer (stratum granulosum)

- Prickle cell layer (stratum spinosum)

- Basal layer (stratum germiniativum)

- *Horny layer* – In this layer, the skin cells are flat. They resemble scales and are composed mainly from keratin. This helps to reflect ultraviolet light from the skin's surface, black skin, which evolved to withstand strong ultraviolet light, has a thicker horny layer than that of Caucasian skin

- *Lucid layer or clear layer* – These cells are clear in appearance. They are found in the non-hairy areas of the body such as the palms of the hands and soles of the feet

- *Granular layer* – Within this layer there is a transition from living to dead cells. Keratinisation, which is the hardening of the skin cells, takes place within this layer

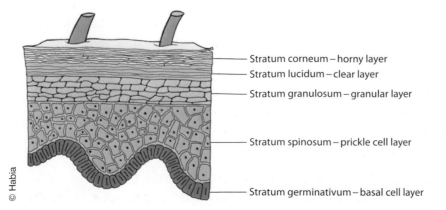

© Habia

Five layers of the skin

Stratum corneum – horny layer
Stratum lucidum – clear layer
Stratum granulosum – granular layer
Stratum spinosum – prickle cell layer
Stratum germinativum – basal cell layer

- *Prickle cell layer* – Named because of the appearance of the cells which have fine, spiky projections. Chemical changes in this layer lead to the eventual keratinisation or hardening of the cells, which makes the skin hard and durable. Two other important cells are found in this layer, the **Langerhan cells** and **melanocyte** cells. Langerhan cells absorb and remove foreign bodies that enter the skin. Melanocyte cells produce the skins pigment **melanin**, which contributes to our skin colour.

  The quantity and distribution of melanocytes are different depending on race. In white Caucasian skin melanin tends to be destroyed when it reaches the granular layer. In black skin melanin is present in larger quantities throughout all the epidermal layers.

- *Basal layer* – The lowest layer of the epidermis. In this layer the cells are constantly dividing by a process known as **mytosis**.

The dermis

The dermis is also known as the 'true skin', and it is within this section that the appendages to the hair and the blood and nerve supply are found along with other structures such as the **lymphatic system**, **blood vessels**, **hair follicles** and **nerves**. The dermis is much thicker than the epidermis and has two main sections: the papillary and the reticular layers.

Papillary layer

This is the outermost layer of the dermis which extends in to the epidermis to supply it with nutrients. Near the surface of the dermis are tiny projections called **papillae**: they contain both nerve endings and blood capillaries.

Reticular layer

The reticular layer is denser and is continuous with the **basement membrane**. In the reticular layer the dermis contains protein fibres: *yellow elastin fibres* which give the skin its elasticity and *white collagen fibres* which give the skin its strength. The fibres are made up from cells called **fibroblasts**.

The basement membrane is not part of the skin, and lies at the base of the dermis. Its purpose is to attach the skin to underlying bone and muscles as well as supplying it with blood vessels and nerves. The dermis contains different types of sensory nerve endings, which register touch, pressure, pain and temperature. These nerve endings send messages to the central nervous system and the brain to inform us about what is happening on the surface of our skin.

A number of structures which we call skin appendages are based within the dermis. These include:

- sweat glands
- sebaceous glands
- hair follicles
- nails

It's a fact! The acid mantle is the term given to the combination of sweat and sebum which creates an acid film on the skin. As the name suggests, it is an acid with a pH of about 4.5–5.5. This film discourages the growth of bacteria and fungi.

Sweat glands are also known as *sudoriferous glands*, which extends into the epidermis from the dermis. Sweat glands are found all over the body but are found in larger amounts on the palms of the hands and the soles of the feet. Their role is to regulate body temperature through the evaporation of sweat from the surface of the skin to stop the body overheating. There are two types of sweat glands:

- **Eccrine glands** are found all over the body and are simple sweat-producing glands that respond to heat. The sweat duct opens onto the surface of the skin through an opening called a **pore**.

- **Apocrine glands** are found in the armpits, the nipples and the groin area. They are connected to hair follicles and become active during puberty. They are larger than the eccrine glands as they secrete a thicker fluid that is made from urea, fats, sugar and small amounts of protein. The gland increases in activity during times of stress, nervousness or excitement. Also found within the fluid are traces of aromatic molecules called **pheromones**, which are thought to create sexual attraction between individuals.

Sebaceous glands are a small sac-like organ. They can be found all over the body except on the palms of the hands and soles of the feet.

This gland is usually associated with the hair follicle and is found in large numbers on the scalp, forehead and the back and chest. They produce the skin's natural oil, **sebum**. Sebum is emptied directly onto the hair follicle.

Cross section of the skin

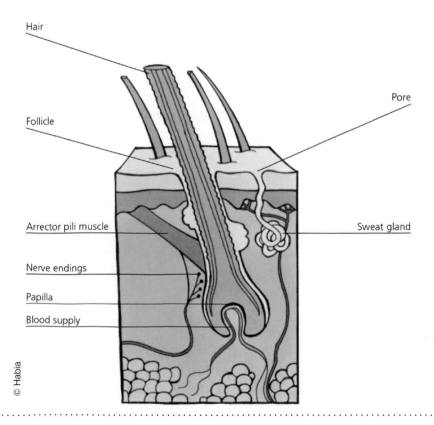

Hair

Pore

Follicle

Arrector pili muscle

Sweat gland

Nerve endings

Papilla

Blood supply

© Habia

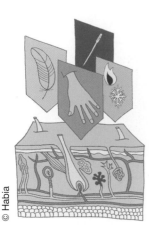

Skin function – sense of touch

© Habia

Skin function – Heat regulation

© Habia

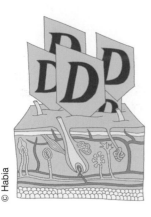

Skin function – absorption

© Habia

Hair follicle

Hair grows from a thin tube in the skin called a hair follicle. The *arrector pili* muscle is attached at the base of the hair follicle. The sebaceous gland is attached to the upper part of the follicle. To find out more about the hair follicle you read about hair structure in Chapter 4, get ahead with hairstyling.

The functions of the skin

The functions of the skin are:

- Sense of touch
- Heat regulation
- Absorption
- Protection
- Excretion and Secretion

- Sense of touch – the dermis contains many sensory nerve endings which can transmit messages to the brain to ensure that you are aware of your surroundings. Sometimes you are able to detect the most minute and delicate feelings. At other times the sense of touch can be much more defined.

- Heat regulation – within the dermis there are many special nerve endings that can detect heat and cold. The organs of the body are designed to work at our normal body temperature of 36.8°C or 98.6°F, so it is important that this temperature is maintained.

- Absorption – while the skin acts as a barrier and prevents harmful micro-organisms entering the body, it is capable of a limited amount of absorption. The skin absorbs vitamin D, which is derived from sunlight. Vitamin D is essential for the body as it helps the formation of healthy bones.

- Protection – the skin is the largest organ of the body and one of its functions is to protect other organs within the body. It does this by creating a barrier around the body which prevents the invasion of **micro-organisms**. The skin is also able to detect danger. It does this by the nerve endings that can track extremes of heat and cold as well as pain from something that may penetrate the surface of the skin – thus protecting the body from harm.

- Excretion – the skin excretes sweat, which helps to dispose of excess salts in the body as well as helping to cool the skin when you are too warm.

- Secretion – the skin also secretes sebum. Sebum helps to moisturise the skin and hair in order to prevent excessive dryness.

Skin types

The term skin *type* describes the appearance of the skin and how it functions. There are four categories:

SKIN TYPE	BASIC FACTS ON THE DIFFERENT SKIN TYPES – CHARACTERISTICS AND APPEARANCE
Normal	• The skins pore size is usually small to medium in size
	• The moisture content is good
	• The skin texture is even, neither too thick nor too thin
	• The colour of the skin looks healthy and has even pigmentation
	• The skin's elasticity is good, when young
	• The skin feels firm to the touch
Dry	• The skins pores are small and tight
	• The skins moisture content is poor
	• Skin texture is coarse and thin, with patches of visibly flaking skin
	• The skin can have a tendency towards sensitivity
	• Premature ageing is common, resulting in the appearance of wrinkles, seen especially around the eyes, mouth and neck.
	• The skins colouring may be uneven, and freckles usually accompany this skin type
	• Milia are often found around the cheek and eye area
Greasy/Oily	• The skins pores are usually enlarged
	• The skins moisture content is high
	• Skin is coarse and thick
	• Skin is sallow in colour, as a result of the excess sebum production, dead skin cells having become embedded in the sebum
	• Skin tone is good, due to the protective effect of the sebum
	• Skin is prone to shininess, due to excess sebum production
	• There may be uneven skin colour
	• Certain skin disorders may be apparent – spots such as comedones, pustules, papules, milia or sebaceous cysts
Combination	• The skin has both oily and dry areas usually in a T-zone. The oily area is usually the T-zone that goes across the forehead, nose and chin. The dry area is usually the cheeks

Skin function – protection

© Habia

Skin function – excretion and secretion

© Habia

It's a fact!

Dermatology is the branch of medicine that is concerned with the skin.

- Pores in the T-zone are enlarged, while in the cheek area they are small to medium

- Moisture content is high in the oily areas, but poor in the dry areas

- Skin is coarse and thick in the oily areas, but thin in the dry areas

- Skin is sallow in the oily areas, but shows sensitivity and high colour in the dry areas

- Skin tone is good in the oily areas, but poor in the dry areas

- There may be blemishes such as pustules and comedones on the oily skin at the T-zone

- Milia and broken capillaries may appear in the dry areas, commonly on the cheeks and near the eyes

ACTIVITY

In groups or pairs discuss the different skin types. Can you identify each others skin type?

Types of skin conditions

Before beginning any service or treatment a professional beauty therapist will examine the client's skin to identify the skin type and any skin condition. This examination is part of the **consultation** process.

Different conditions tend to display different symptoms; in the charts below you will learn to recognise the different skin, conditions that you may come across as a professional beauty therapist when carrying out a consultation.

Viral conditions

Viruses are groups of very simple organisms that are smaller than bacteria and can cause infections and disease.

CONDITION	CAUSE AND SYMPTOMS	TREATMENT
Cold sores 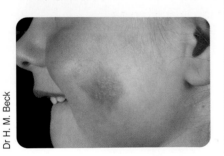 Dr H. M. Beck	An infectious condition that appears when the skin has been exposed to extremes in temperature or by ultraviolet light (sunlight). It can also appear when a person's resistance is low through ill health or stress. At first the skin's condition appears inflamed and red in a localised areas such as on the cheek or lips. Then the area can become itchy and a crust forms that often cracks and weeps fluid	This is a recurring skin condition that is difficult to treat. Medical treatment should be sought and treatments and services should not take place on the skin near the area of infection

Warts

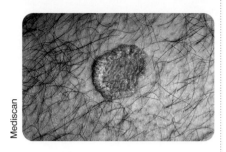

Mediscan

Warts are infectious outgrowths of the epidermis and can be found anywhere on the body. They appear as small roughened areas of skin that form lumps. They can vary in colour from a pale flesh colour to brown. The virus is more easily spread through water, so shampooing a client with warts on their head may lead to the transfer of the virus

Medical treatment should be sought and treatments and services should not be carried out in the area infected

Bacterial conditions

Bacteria are a large group of micro-organisms many of which can cause infection and disease.

CONDITION	CAUSE AND SYMPTOMS	TREATMENT
Impetigo 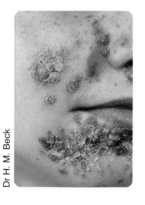 Dr H. M. Beck	Impetigo is a infectious condition were bacteria enters an opening of the skin causing a burning sensation, which is followed by yellow spots and pustules filled with clear fluid, which dry into yellow or honey-coloured crusty formations. The condition can be found on any area of the body but usually appears on the face and scalp. Impetigo can be spread by direct or indirect contact by a person or through dirty tools and towels	Medical treatment should be sought and treatments and services should not be carried out in the infected area
Conjunctivitis  Wellcome Images	Conjunctivitis is an infectious condition of the eye which inflames the mucous membrane that covers the eye and lines the eyelid. The eye becomes sore and red and pus can sometimes be excreted	Medical treatment should be sought and treatments and services should not be carried out in the infected area

Fungal conditions

Fungi are microscopic plants that do not have leaves or roots. Fungal infections of the skin live off waste products produced by the skin.

CONDITION	CAUSE AND SYMPTOMS	TREATMENT
Ringworm First published in *The World of Hair*, J.E. Gray, Macmillan Press, 1997	This condition is not caused by a worm, as the name suggests, but a fungus that lives on the keratin of the skin and hair. The symptoms are patches of pink skin surrounded by a red active ring. The centre of the patch is covered in grey scales of dead keratin and if on the scalp the hair will break leaving stubble	Medical treatment should be sought and treatments and services should not be carried out in the infected area

Parasitic conditions

This is when an animal or plant lives on or in our body so that it can feed.

CONDITION	CAUSE AND SYMPTOMS	TREATMENT
Scabies Dr M. H. Beck	This condition is caused by the itch mite. The mite called *Sarcoptes Scabiei* burrows through the skin leaving greyish lines and reddish spots. The condition is extremely itchy, particularly at night. Scabies is contagious and can be passed on by close physical contact	Medical treatment should be sought and treatments and services should not be carried out

Skin care products

You need to use the best and most effective products for your skin type. We all know that we can buy beauty products from the high street. The question is why we would buy our products off the shelf with no knowledge of what they are and why we are buying them?

Let us look at some of the advantages and disadvantages of buying products in both a retail shop or in a beauty salon.

ADVANTAGES OF BUYING PRODUCTS IN A RETAIL SHOP	DISADVANTAGES OF BUYING IN A RETAIL SHOP
Lots of choice	Not knowing which products to buy
Often have cheaper products or special offers on products	People often buy the cheaper products but they may not be the best product to achieve the desired result
	No specialist to ask or give advice

ADVANTAGES OF BUYING IN A PROFESSIONAL SALON	DISADVANTAGES OF BUYING IN A PROFESSIONAL SALON
Salons specialise in a limited range of products	Not always a large stock and products may not always be available
Product range is used for both professional use and for retail	Can be more expensive than buying on the high street
Professional people to give advice on how and when to use the product for best results	

Now let's look at the skin care products that you can choose from.

Cleansers

There are a variety of cleansers that can be used depending on your skin type.

- *Cleaning lotion* – a strong **astringent**-type cleanser that is more effective for oily and congested skins.

- *Cleaning milk* – a gentler, milky type that is effective on young skin types but may be too drying for older skins.

- *Cleansing cream* – a heavier type of cleanser, more effective for dry and mature skins.

- *Foaming cleanser* – becomes a mousse when mixed with water-effective on combination and oily skins.

Cleanser

Toner

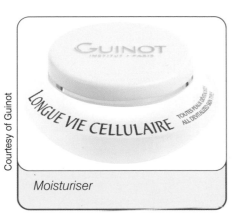

Moisturiser

Facial scrub/exfoliant

Toners

Toners can vary in strength but all are designed to refresh the skin, remove any remains of cleanser and tighten pores.

- *Fresheners* – very mild, best for dry and mature skins

- *Toners* – slightly stronger than fresheners with a mild astringent effect, most effective on normal skin.

- *Astringent* – very strong as it contains alcohol, and sometimes **antiseptic**. Best for combination and oil skins

Moisturisers

A moisturiser is necessary to prevent the skin from drying out and becoming dehydrated. In addition, it is used to protect the skin from harsh elements such as strong winds, sun, central heating or air conditioning.

- *Moisturising lotion* a lighter product best suited to young and oily skins.

- *Moisturising mousse* a lighter 'whipped' cream consistency ideally suited for normal skin types.

- *Moisturising cream* heavier and richer, better for dry and mature skins.

Facial scrubs

This is a special product designed to remove dead skin cells (exfoliate) and to make the skin appear brighter, clearer and glowing. If the dead skin cells are removed then products can be absorbed more quickly into the skin.

Most facial scrubs consist of a cream that contains fine particles that are abrasive and so slough off the dead skin cells. Another type of scrub is one where the product is brushed on to the face, left to dry out, then massaged off. The product ends up as 'crumbs' and dead skin cells are once again sloughed off with the massaging technique.

Face masks

Face masks are a special treatment designed to give a more concentrated effect on certain skin types and conditions. They can reinforce the effects of cleansing, or enhance the moisture content of the skin; it all depends on the choice of mask.

There are two types of mask:

- *Setting masks* – usually applied thinly and then they dry out, causing a tightening sensation.

- *Non-setting mask* – They are the most popular type in the salon, and the type you will apply as part of your Diploma in Hair and Beauty Studies. There are many type of masks available, and almost every skin care range offers at least one. Some are for oily troubled skin, others for dehydrated and ageing skin, and even 'brightening' masks for dull sallow skin.

Bring your learning to life

When you are on your work placement or in a salon environment, find out about the different types of skin care treatments that are available for the client. Produce a simple leaflet that explains what each treatment does.

Looking after your skin

Do you have a healthy lifestyle? How busy are you? Do you do everything you can to have healthy glowing skin?

When considering your skin care routine it's important to look at your lifestyle. How you live your life can show on your skin. Usually if you eat a healthy balanced diet, drink plenty of water, take regular exercise and get lots of fresh air, your skin will be clear and glowing with good health.

It's a fact!

Your skin can be affected by many factors, including

Poor nutrition	Smoking	Alcohol
Stress	Medication/drugs	Illness
Hormonal changes	Extreme weather	Poor skin care
Central heating	Sunburn	Lack of fresh air

A simple but effective routine is best, so that it fits neatly into your everyday habits, and remember it only takes 30 days to start a habit. Your skin care routine should be as easy as brushing your teeth, done twice a day to get the best results … glowing skin!

EXTEND YOUR LEARNING

A healthy lifestyle will give you healthy skin. Find out what effects the following can have on your skin:

- Lifestyle
- The environment

Produce a short report on your findings.

Bring your learning to life

Write a daily diary of your activities for one week. Include in the diary the following information:

- What time you get up and what you did before going out

- What you did during the day

- What you did in the evening

- What time you went to sleep

At the end of the week review the information that you have written. Can you see a pattern to your activities? Do you think your activities help promote healthy skin? Do you think you have a skin care routine? If not, do you have time to develop a skin care routine? Write down what you would include in your skin care routine. If you have a skin care routine do you think it needs improving? How would you improve it?

For the next four weeks include your new or adapted skin care routine into your daily activities. At the end of the four weeks write a simple report on your findings. Did your skin look and feel better or not?

Preparing the treatment area for a client

When preparing the treatment area for a facial treatment you will need to ensure the environment is suitable. Make sure the room is prepared.

- The temperature is nice and warm, but not too stuffy.

- The lighting should be soft, so that it is relaxing for the person having the facial.

- Fragranced candles can enhance the atmosphere, and make it a more relaxed setting.

- Use suitable background music.

Equipment and materials

It is good practice to make sure you have all the equipment you need ready and prepared before you start a treatment. For the facial treatment you need to have the following items ready for the client;

1 Linen/duvet/blankets - clean bedding to keep the person protected and warm.

2 Towels - clean, soft, fluffy towels.

3 Clean gown/bathrobe - for the client's modesty and comfort.

4 Lined swing wastebin - essential for hygienically disposing of waste.

5 Steriliser - essential for ensuring equipment and tools are sterile, to prevent the spread of infection.

Set up your treatment area with the following specialised equipment.

EQUIPMENT	USE	BENEFITS
Treatment bed/couch/beauty chair	A comfortable bed on which the treatment is carried out. It needs to be easy to clean	Can be adjusted to suit the comfort of the individual, so they relax during the treatment. A hydraulic bed that can be lowered makes it easier to get on
Equipment trolley	Specially designed trolley/table with shelves to hold all the tools and products. Should be easy to clean	Easy to move around the bed, so your tools and products are all in one place, and close at hand
Beauty stool/chair	A special chair/stool designed for carrying out beauty treatments	Much easier to perform treatments, it is comfortable, with an adjustable height and has a back rest

On your trolley make sure you have prepared the following;

1 Spatulas - clean spatulas used to remove product from jars or containers.

2 Bowls - selection of sizes, usually to hold jewellery, cotton wool and water for mask removal.

3 Headband - protects and keeps hair secure, and out of the way of facial products.

4 Removal sponges - sterilised sponges to remove the face mask.

5 Cotton wool (dry and damp) - prepare plenty of cotton wool for the entire treatment.

6 Cotton buds - necessary for removing any makeup close to the lashes.

7 Tissues - prepare plenty, to last the entire treatment.

8 Mask brush - a specialised brush for applying the mask to the face and neck

9 Hand mirror - essential for consulting with the client whilst analysing the skin type, during and at the end of the facial.

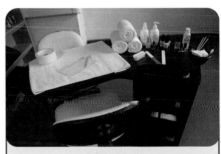

Select all the products you need

In addition you need to make sure you have the following skincare products on your trolley.

1 Eye makeup remover

2 Skin cleanser

3 Skin toner

4 Moisturiser

5 Scrub

6 Face mask

ACTIVITY

Work on your own or as part of a team. Collect information on different skin care products, what they are and how they work. Use the information to carry out an informative presentation.

Carrying out a skin care routine

Now that you are aware of all the factors that affect the appearance and condition of the skin, and you know how to select the right products and tools – you're ready to put the theory into practice!

The five basic steps are:

Step 1: cleansing

Cleansing is one of the most important stages in the skin care routine. Many people feel the key to great-looking skin is how clean it is, and how it glows with health and vitality. Skin that isn't cleansed thoroughly can look dirty, dull, tired, with blemishes such as blackheads and spots.

There are two parts to the cleansing routine:

1 Superficial cleansing to remove makeup and surface grease and dirt.

2 Deep cleansing to give a deeper cleanse to the face, removing every trace of dirt to ensure the skin is squeaky clean.

Superficial cleansing
The routine for the superficial cleanse is:

- Eyes/lashes

- Lips

- Face and neck

Top tip Male skin care - don't use cotton wool pads to remove products as it gets caught in the strong facial hair. Use dampened sponges instead.

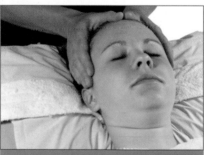

1 Wash your hands, and dry thoroughly. Apply pressure to the scalp, to start the relaxation process. Ensure the headband is firmly in place to protect the hair.

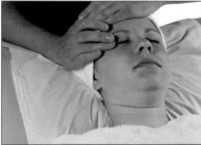

2 Cleanse each eye separately. Start with the right eye, apply eye makeup remover in small circular movements over the eyelid and lashes. Ensure the pressure is very light. Always support the eyebrow area with your free hand. Repeat on the left eye.

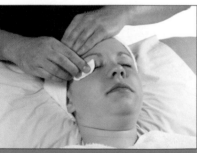

3 Take damp cotton wool pads and stroke the pads down over the lid and lashes, until all the eye makeup has been removed.

4 If necessary use a cotton bud to get the last traces of eye shadow and mascara off.

5 Cleanse each side of the lips separately. Apply a cleaning lotion or milk in small circles to the right side of the mouth, supporting the corner of the mouth with your free hand.

6 Take damp cotton wool pads, and stroke inwards across the lips to remove all lipstick, repeat until the lips are clean.

7 Apply the cleanser to the face and start at the forehead with light strokes.

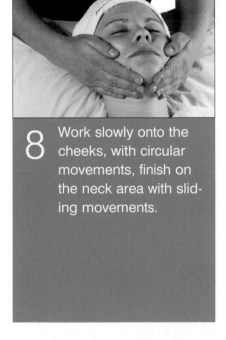

8 Work slowly onto the cheeks, with circular movements, finish on the neck area with sliding movements.

9 With damp cotton wool pads in each hand, remove the cleanser with light upward strokes. Facial sponges can also be used to remove the cleanser. Repeat until all the cleanser is removed.

Deep cleanse

The deep cleansing procedure involves a routine of 10 massage movements, to help the cleansing product be absorbed deep into the pores and follicles to ensure the skin is cleaned thoroughly.

Choose a cleanser that is suitable for the skin type. Apply to both your hands evenly, and then apply to the face and neck in long flowing strokes. Then take 10 minutes to go through the following nine massage strokes:

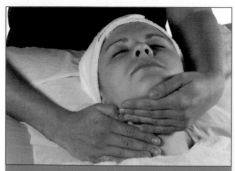

1 Stroking (neck area) – using your fingertips stroke up both sides of the neck, then outward under the jaw, and back down lightly to the starting position.

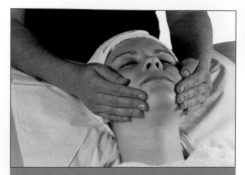

2 Finger kneading to the chin area.

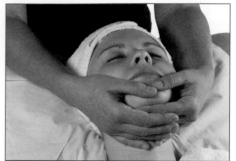

3 Thumb kneading to the entire chin area.

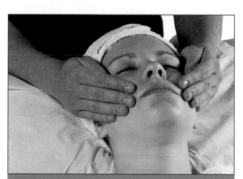

4 Circling (cheek area) – apply small circles with fingertips to entire cheek area, starting at the chin, working up around the nose, across the cheekbone and back along lower cheek to chin.

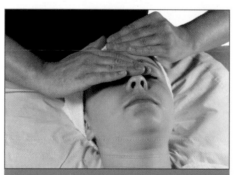

5 Gliding (nose) – with ring and middle fingers of right hand, start at base of nose and glide along the length of the nose and off the end, followed by the left hand.

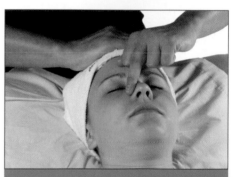

6 Circling (eye area) – with middle finger circle around each eye. Start on the inner eyebrow, stroke out along brow bone and inwards under the eye. Adapt to form a 'figure 8' movement, with each hand working alternatively.

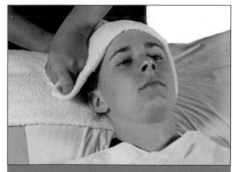

7 Circling (forehead) – with ring and middle fingers perform small circles across the forehead.

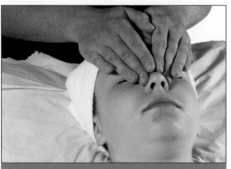

8 Sliding (eye area) – with index, middle and ring fingers, slide outwards around the brow bone and underneath the eye area. At the end of the stroke, lift and apply pressure with each individual finger on the brow bone.

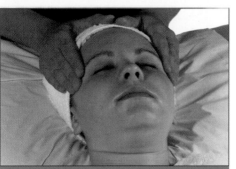

9 Circling (temple area) – with the index, middle and ring fingers circle on the temple area, applying slight pressure. Pause at the end, and hold for a count of 3.

Step 2: facial scrub

Application of scrub:

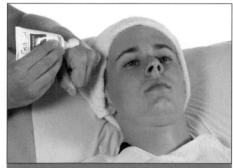

1 Place the clean towel on the pillow, and wrap the towel carefully over the head, protecting the hairline.

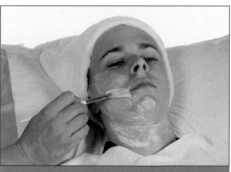

2 Choose the appropriate scrub for the skin type. Always read and follow the manufacturer's instructions carefully. Place a small amount of scrub on the back of your hand.

3 Apply the scrub to the face with a mask brush. Explain to the client the sensation they will feel.

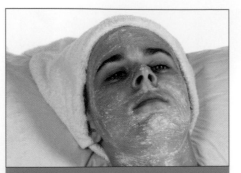

4 Make sure the scrub is applied evenly all over the neck, chin, cheeks, nose and forehead.

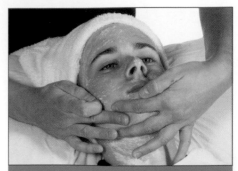

5 With small circular motions, lightly massage the entire face and neck in an upwards direction. Be careful on delicate areas such as the cheeks and avoid the eye area and lips. If the scrub dries out too much, and starts to drag, add water by dampening your hands.

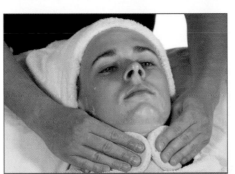

6 The scrub is left on the skin for the recommended time, according to the manufacturer's instructions. Use warm damp sponges to remove the scrub, starting at the neck, make sure you check the hairline and around the nostrils. Do not have the sponges too wet or it will be uncomfortable for the client.

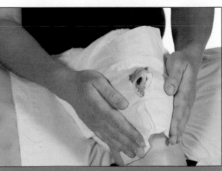

7 Blot the face with a tissue.

Step 3: face mask

Application of a setting mask:

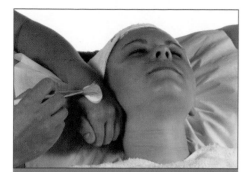

1 Choose the appropriate mask for the skin type. Always read and follow the manufacturer's instructions carefully. Apply a small amount of mask to the back of your hand.

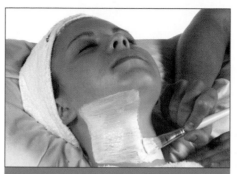

2 Using a clean mask brush apply the mask quickly so the skin gets the maximum effect from the active ingredients in the mask. Start at the base of the neck.

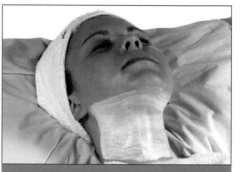

3 It is important to apply the mask quickly and evenly so it doesn't dry out sooner in some parts of the face or neck, as it could irritate the skin. Explain to the client the sensation they will feel.

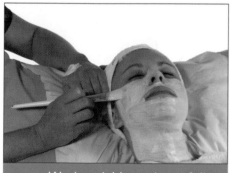

4 Work quickly and carefully upwards, avoid the lips, nostrils, eye area and eyebrows.

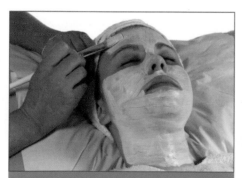

5 Finish on the forehead, being careful to avoid the hairline.

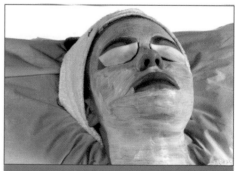

6 Dampened cotton wool pads are applied to the eyes, this helps to relax the client. The mask is left on the skin for the recommended time, according to the manufacturer's instructions.

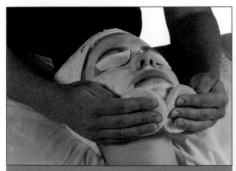

7 Use warm damp sponges to remove the mask, starting on the neck area. Do not forget to remove the eye pads and continue on to the cheek area. Do not have the sponges too wet or it will be uncomfortable for the client.

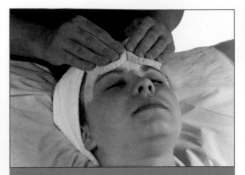

8 Be careful to remove every last trace of the mask, which can be a challenge with a 'setting' mask.

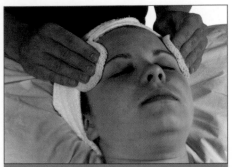

9 Check the hairline, around the nostrils and under the chin to ensure there are no traces of mask left on the skin.

Application of a non-setting mask:

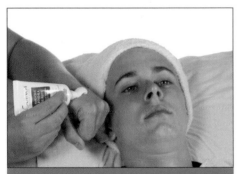

1 Choose the appropriate mask for the skin type. Always read and follow the manufacturer's instructions carefully. Apply a small amount of mask to the back of your hand.

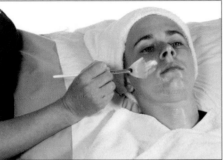

2 Using a clean mask brush apply the mask quickly so the skin gets the maximum effect from the active ingredients in the mask. Start at the base of the neck and work carefully upwards, finishing on the forehead. Avoid the lips, nostrils, eye area, eyebrows and hairline. Apply the mask evenly so it doesn't dry out earlier in some parts of the face or neck. Explain to the client the sensation they will feel.

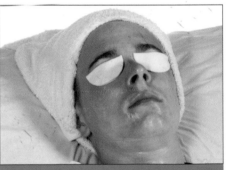

3 Dampened cotton wool pads are applied to the eyes, this helps to relax the client. The mask is left on the skin for the recommended time, according to the manufacturer's instructions.

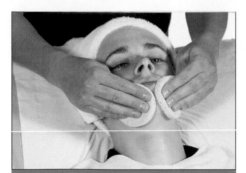

4 Remove the eye pads, and use warm damp sponges to remove the mask. Do not have the sponges too wet or it will be uncomfortable for the client. Be careful to remove every last trace of the mask, which can be a challenge, check the hairline, around the nostrils and under the chin.

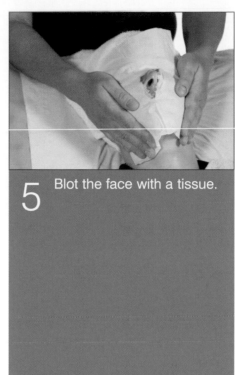

5 Blot the face with a tissue.

Top tip

Toner can be applied as a 'mist' using a vapouriser, which can be both relaxing and refreshing for the client.

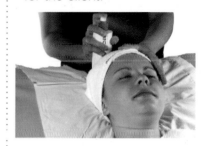

Step 4: toning

Application of toner:

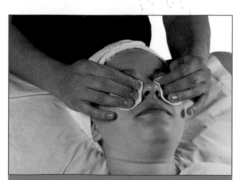

1 Choose the appropriate toner for the skin type. Apply the toner to two damp cotton wool pads. Starting at the base of the neck, wipe the pads gently over the neck and face using long sweeping, flowing strokes.

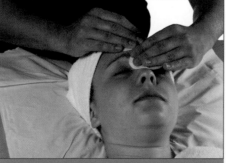

2 Continue over the entire face.

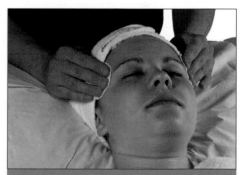

3 Repeat if necessary, until the skin is free of grease or product.

4 Blot the skin to remove any excess toner. Take a facial tissue, tear a small hole in the middle for the nose, apply to the face, and gently press all over to absorb any excess toner.

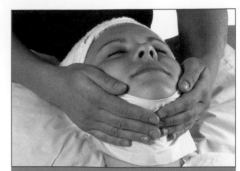

5 Remove the tissue, fold in half and apply to the neck area, and gently press.

Step 5: moisturising

Application of moisturiser:

1 Ensure there is no excess toner on the skin, and that a tissue has been used to blot the face and neck.

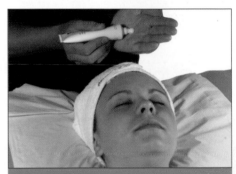

2 Choose the correct moisturiser for the skin type.

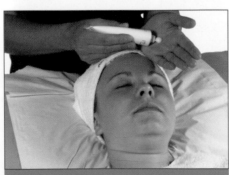

3 Place a small amount of moisturiser in the palm of your hand.

4 Apply the moisturiser sparingly to the neck, chin, cheeks, nose and forehead.

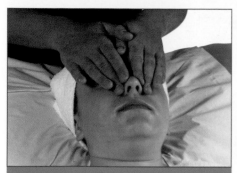

5 Lightly massage the moisturiser into the face and neck with upwards and outwards flowing strokes.

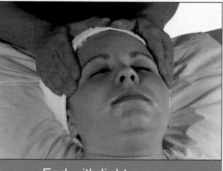

6 End with light pressure on the temples.

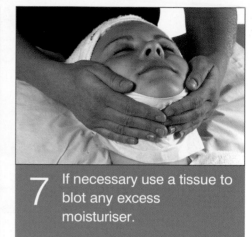

7 If necessary use a tissue to blot any excess moisturiser.

What you have learnt

- The perceptions of facial beauty:
  - How beauty is seen differently by people
- Skin structure and skin conditions:
  - The different layers of the skin
  - The different functions of the skin
  - How the appearance of skin differs
  - The different types of skin conditions that can affect the skin
  - How they are caused and how you can recognise the symptoms
- Preparation needed for carrying out skin care routines:
  - The different types of skin products available
  - Preparing the treatment area ready for a client
  - The types of equipment and tools that will be needed
- Skin care routines and treatments:
  - Looking after your own skin
  - Carrying out a skin care routine

Assessment activities

Crossword

Across

2 Used to stop the skin drying out (11)

5 Type of cleaner used on greasy/oily skin (5)

6 Term used to explain the combination of sweat and sebum (4, 6)

8 Product used to remove dead skin cells (5)

Down

1 Used to refresh the skin (6)

3 The outer layer of the skin (9)

4 A habit that effects the condition of your skin (7)

7 A skin type (6)

9 The client lays on it (3)

Wordsearch

```
A W Y M R D J Q X B K Y P C X M X
K R A L T E Z V B R I D Z T Z O N
M S Y I I J N Y G U P J G A W Z Y
K M E F H O C O B S M I R R E A W
M I E E L J G U T H W Z X B O W L
O R N S I I A L U T A P S B I M K
I R I T R O N S I M R E D I P E W
S O T Y I H B H Y N O R M A L M Q
T R U L C L E A N E R C U G W V I
U S O E A A P L N S K C B M A X H
R E R U L V M O B J C U E C N S J
I P I T O Y D Y K H P R S S V L Z
S V H X O E B T J E H F U J A M C
E N C O M B I N A T I O N B Y N S
R R B O M V O W W M S S L L P U G
A K C F Y E G F C K R P F B L J H
L I T Z I O E L B S P O N G E S L
```

Dermis	Scrub	Normal	Bowl
Epidermis	Moisturiser	Combination	Sponges
Cleaner	Comedone	Routine	Brush
Toner	Sebum	Health	Mirror
Mask	Oily	Spatula	Lifestyle

The five layers of the epidermis

Label the diagram.

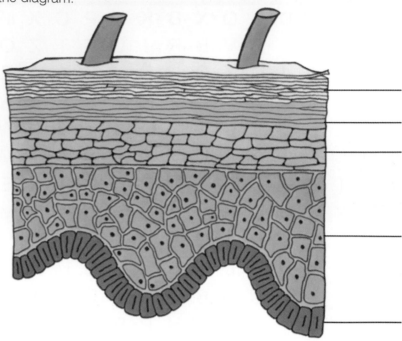

Cross-section of the skin

Label the diagram.

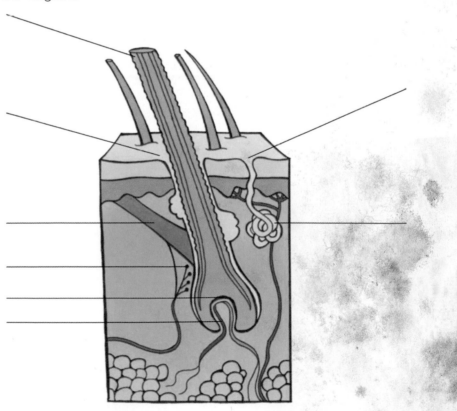

Skin types

Link the skin types on the left with the skin characteristics on the right. You may use different coloured markers to show your connections.

Skin types

Skin characteristics

Dry

Well-balanced skin

Spots can be present

Greasy/oily

Lack of sebum and moisture

Oily and dry areas

Combination

High level of sebum produced

Skin can feel quite rough to the touch

Normal

Usually has a T-zone

Good skin texture

6
nailing it

When you're finished changing, you're finished

BENJAMIN FRANKLIN AMERICAN INVENTOR

Introduction

The quote above says '*When you're finished changing, you're finished.* 'The hair and beauty industries are continually changing – and so will never be finished. One major change has been with the nail industry.

Have you noticed the number of nail salons you see now? There are many more than there were even 5 years ago. You will see there is at least one nail salon on almost every high street.

What you are going to learn

In this chapter you will learn about:

★ Why the appearance of hands and nails is important

★ The structure of the nails and skin

★ The main factors affecting nail care services

★ Skin and nail conditions that affect services and treatments

★ Basic hand care and nail treatments

★ How to prepare for hand and nail treatments

★ How to carry out a basic hand and nail treatment

★ The technological developments in nail services

★ The terminology related to hand and nail care services

You can have a career just working with nails. If you love nails, and that's what you want to specialise in, then you can study and become qualified in a wide range of nail services.

In this chapter you will learn about the skills and knowledge that will help you care for your hands and nails. If you develop these skills and study further, you can become a professional nail technician.

The importance of hand and nail care

People often say they can tell a lot about a person by their hands. What do your nails and hands say about you? Do they say 'I care for my hands and nails and look after them'? Or do they say 'I neglect my hands and nails and hide them if others are likely to see them'.

A **manicure** involves the care of the hands and fingernails.

It's a fact!

ACTIVITY

This can be a whole class activity, or you can work with a partner.

You can tell a lot about a person from their hands. Discuss what you think about the appearance of the nails in photograph A and photograph B.

Discuss the following:

- What do you think the person would be like who has the nails in photograph A?

- What do you think the person would be like who has the nails in photograph B?

- Do you think there would be a situation when the person in photograph A would be limited in what they can do?

- Do you think that there would be a situation when the person with the nails in photograph B may not want others to see them?

You should be able to see from the activity that you don't always need long, extended nails, but you do have to have nails that suit your lifestyle and provide a positive image about you.

Photograph A

© iStockphoto.com/Valua Vitaly

Photograph B

© iStockphoto.com/George Peters

Your lifestyle can be reflected in your hands and nails. Perhaps you are a nervous person, and chew your nails. Or maybe you are someone who likes everything to be perfect, and has very neat, perfectly manicured and polished nails.

Looking at the condition of the hands and nails does not give you the full story of someone's life, but it's a start. Hands are very visual. They are always on show.

So you need to be confident about how your hands and nails look.

Nail care for men

Nail and hand care is not just for females. Men are also getting interested. More and more are having regular manicures and wearing nail enamel.

Rock bands probably popularised the wearing of nail enamel. The colours were usually very dark, or black. In 1997 the cosmetic company Hard Candy developed 'Candy Man' a nail enamel brand aimed at men. The colours were called *Testosterone* (gunmetal grey), *Gigolo* (silver-specked black), *Superman* (dark blue) and *Dog* (deep purple).

ACTIVITY

Investigate how many of your male friends and relatives have hand treatment or nail services – either professionally, or done by themselves.

EXTEND YOUR LEARNING

 Look at this website and see the nail treatments that are available for men: http://www.martynmaxey.co.uk/men.php. You could also investigate if your local nail salons offer special hand or nail care services for men.

Nails and your health

As well as lifestyle, your health can also be reflected in your nails. If you eat an unhealthy diet, you can't expect your hands to be soft and smooth, or your nails to be strong.

To be able to care for the hands and nails and improve their appearance, you need to know about the structure of the nail and its function.

Nail structure

Nails are found on the ends of your fingers and toes and they protect the ends of your fingers or toes. They also protect small bones from knocks and damage. You can also use your nails to pick up small, delicate objects.

The nail is made from **keratin**. This is the same protein that hair and skin is made of. There are special chains of keratin in the nails that make them hard.

The nail unit is made up of three main parts:

- **Nail bed**
- **Matrix**
- **Nail plate**

Nail bed

The nail bed is the living skin on which the **nail plate** sits. The nail bed is supplied with blood vessels that give the nail plate a pinkish appearance. The nail bed is supplied with many nerves and is attached to the nail plate by a thin layer of tissue called the **bed epithelium**. The bed epithelium acts as a seal against infection for that area of the nail and also helps to guide the nail plate along the nail bed as it grows.

Matrix

The matrix is where the nail plate is formed.

It extends from under the nail fold at the base of the nail plate. The visible part of the matrix which can be seen at the base of the nail plate is called the **lunula**. You can see this as a curve or half-moon shape, which is lighter than the rest of the nail plate.

Nail plate

The nail plate is the visible and functional part of the nail unit. It is a hard keratin plate that is based on top of the nail bed. The nail plate is made up of many layers of nail cells.

The section of the nail plate that extends past the bed is called the **free edge**. Attached around the edge of the nail plate is the dead colourless tissue called the **cuticle**. The cuticle comes from the underside of the skin and its job is to seal the space between the nail plate and living skin to prevent the entry of micro-organisms.

Eponychium

The **eponychium** is the living skin at the base of the nail plate covering the matrix area. Sometimes people can confuse the eponychium with the cuticle - but they are not the same. The cuticle is the *dead* tissue on the nail plate, the eponychium is *living* tissue.

Structure of the nail

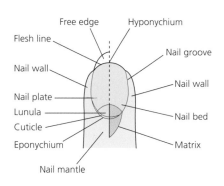

It's a fact! Nails are formed very early in the development of an unborn baby and will be fully formed by week 20.

Cross-section of the nail

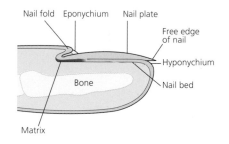

It's a fact! Did you know that the nail can absorb more water than the skin?

Hyponychium

The **hyponychium** is the slightly thickened layer of skin that lies underneath the free edge of the nail plate. The hyponychium creates a seal to prevent micro-organisms infecting the nail bed.

Ligament

A **ligament** is a tough band of tissue that connects bones or holds organs in place. Ligaments attach the nail bed and matrix to the finger bone.

Nail folds

Nail folds are folds of normal skin that surround the nail plate, they form the nail grooves, which are the slits or furrows on the sides of the nail on which the nail moves as it grows.

Free edge

The free edge is the section of the nail that extends beyond the fingertip. It is this section of nail that is filed and shaped. Its function is to protect the fingertip.

Nail growth

The average rate that a nail grows in an adult is about 3.7 mm per month. The growth of the nail plate can be affected by your nutrition, and your health.

If you hurt your nails, or you have a nail disease in the matrix, the shape or thickness of the nail plate can change. If you lose a nail it will take between 4–6 months to replace a fingernail and about 9–12 months to replace a toenail.

Nail shapes

Have you ever noticed the differences in nail shape? A normal, healthy nail can grow in a variety of shapes, depending on the shape of the matrix. A long matrix produces a thicker nail plate and a highly curved matrix creates a highly curved free edge.

If you go to a professional nail technician they will assess the natural shape of your nails before they begin a nail service. They will make sure that the shape of the finished nail will suit the shape and length of your hands. The shape and length of the nail should also suit your lifestyle.

It's a fact! Nails grow faster:

- On hands rather than on feet
- In children and young people rather than older people
- In the summer rather than in the winter
- In pregnancy

ACTIVITY

Compare the natural shape of your nails with those of other people in your class. Who has long thin nails and who has short round ones? Who has a curved free edge and who has a flat free edge? Who has thick, strong nails, and who had thin, weak nails?

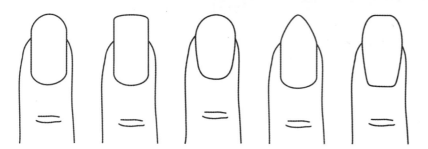

Nail shapes (round, square, oval, pointed, squoval)

The advantages and disadvantages of different nail shapes

NAIL SHAPE	ADVANTAGES	DISADVANTAGES
Round	Ideal for short nails, and for men. Can suit square-shaped hands as it can soften the angular lines	Will not suit large round hands, as it will make them appear much bigger
Square	Suitable for people who do a lot of work with their hands. For example, manual workers, those who use computer keyboards. The shape can be flattering for long thin fingers	Will not suit square-shaped hands as it highlights the angular lines
Oval	Flattering for small hands and short stubby fingers as the shape can appear to lengthen the fingers	Can accentuate long thin bony fingers and hands
Pointed	May be suitable for special occasions – for dramatic effect	Can make long thin bony fingers look aggressive. Can be more prone to break as the nail is weakened at the sides
Squoval	A square shape with curved corners can be very flattering on long slim fingers; can appear more attractive than a regular oval shape	Will not suit square-shaped hands as it can emphasise the angular lines

It's a fact!

Square shaped nails can often be very angular, so to make them more attractive file them with a slight curve at the corners – this is what is known as a **squoval**, and it is a very popular shape.

Dark nail enamel can be very dramatic

© iStockphoto.com/Famke Backx

Why nails are important to the hair and beauty industries

Once, nail treatments were an 'add on' to other hair and beauty treatments and services. Now you can go to a specially trained expert in nail services – a nail technician.

Nails and fashion

Some people like to follow the latest fashions for clothes, hair, makeup. Many also like to follow the fashions for nails. Nail enamel can often complete the *total look*. It can enhance your outfit and your overall style.

The fashion for nail length and shape as well as the nail enamel colour will change. Sometimes it is fashionable for very natural pale colours (even white) on short nails. Then, later it is longer, square-shaped, dark, hot chocolate coloured nails.

Nails and personality

Your personality can all be expressed through the hands, feet and even through **nail art**.

If you are very quiet and shy you may prefer to have short natural nails, avoiding bright nail enamel. But you may be a very confident, bubbly person with an extrovert personality. You may want to express yourself through the appearance of your nails. For example, you may choose to have long nails, painted dark blue with silver stars.

Nail enamel can reflect your personality

© iStockphoto.com/knape

Factors affecting nail care services

There are certain factors that affect hand and nail care and should be taken into consideration before treatments can take place. Professional nail technicians ensure that they are aware of these factors, so that the advice and treatment given are suitable for the client and will enhance the appearance of the hands and nails.

The factors are:

- Occasion
- Lifestyle
- Skin condition/type
- Allergies
- Nail shape
- Skin and nail conditions that may affect hand care services

It's a fact! The word manicure stems from the Latin for 'hand' (*manus*) and 'care' (*cūra*).

Occasion

The look of the nails must be right for the occasion. A professional nail technician will ask their clients questions to find out if they are having a treatment for a particular occasion. Their clients may be having a nail treatment because they are attending an interview. They will want to look very smart and groomed and their nails to look neat, in good condition and well cared for.

Some may be getting married and want their hands and nails to look their best, but very natural. Others may be going to a fancy dress party – perhaps as a Thai dancer with long intricate jewelled nails.

Lifestyle

A professional nail technician will always ask questions about the client's lifestyle.

Working in certain professions means that some people are not allowed to wear nail enamel at all, for example, those that work in a sterile environment such as surgeons, nurses or chefs.

Skin condition

If the skin is dry, this will affect the condition of the nail and cuticle. The cuticles will be very dry, flaky and could split, which may lead to infection. Dehydrated nails would be very flaky and may start to peel in layers. To improve the condition of the skin gloves should be worn when washing up and a good quality hand cream or oil should be massaged into the hands and nails every night. Regular manicures would also help.

Nail treatments are very popular for brides

iStockphoto.com/Megan Lorenz

EXTEND YOUR LEARNING

 Research to find out what nail and hand care services are available for improving the condition of the skin of the hands and the nails.

Top tip

Try looking at the websites for Bliss Spa, **http://www.blisslondon.co.uk** and Nails Inc., **http://www.nailsinc.com**

Allergies

Some people may have an allergic reaction to the products that are used for hand and nail care treatments. For example there could be a reaction to lanolin, enamel remover, acetone, and the perfume in hand lotion or to the nail enamel.

Nail shape

Many different nail shapes can be achieved. The natural shape of the nail should be considered when deciding on the final look. It will be impossible to achieve long sleek pointed nails if the natural shape of the nail is very wide and square.

Skin and nail conditions that may affect hand care services

Contraindications

A **contraindication** is a condition that prevents a treatment from being carried out.

Contraindications can be divided into three categories:

1 *General* – contraindications that affect the entire body.

2 *Local* – contraindications that only involve a *local* area of the hand or nail. For example, scar tissue. A manicure could be carried out providing the area is avoided.

3 *Temporary* – contraindications that are not permanent. Treatment can be carried out once the condition clears up. For example, the client may have a cut or swelling.

Disease and disorders of the hands and nails

There are some diseases and disorders of the hands and nails which mean that treatments and services must not take place at all. This is because the infection could be passed from one person to another.

The hand and nail diseases can be:

- Bacterial

- Viral

- Fungal

- Parasites

CONDITION	CAUSE AND SYMPTOMS	TREATMENT
Viral conditions 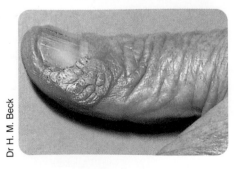 Dr H. M. Beck	Small roughened areas of skin that form lumps. They can vary in colour from a pale flesh colour to brown. Can be found anywhere on the body, including the hands and feet	• Easily spread by water, so if present on hands, manicure services should not take place • Refer for medical advice

Verruca

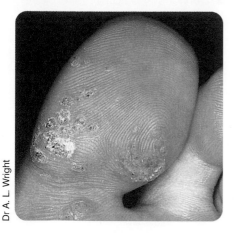

Dr A. L. Wright

Similar to a wart, except that they grow into the skin and usually have black spot in the centre

- Easily spread by water, so if present on feet, pedicure services should not take place

- Refer for medical advice

Bacterial condition

Boils or furuncles

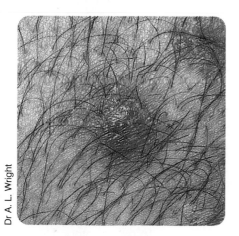

Dr A. L. Wright

Infectious red painful swellings with a hard pus-filled core that extends down into the skin. Boils are formed around the hair follicle and can be found on the wrist and other parts of the body

- Services should not take place while the infection is present in the area of the hands and wrist

- Refer for medical advice

Fungal conditions

Ringworm of the nail plate

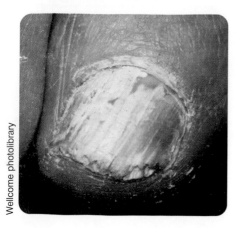

Wellcome photolibrary

Infectious condition caused by fungal infection. The nail plate will become a yellowish–grey colour, the nail plate will become dry and brittle and eventually separate from the nail bed

- Services should not take place while the infection is present on the nails

- Refer for medical advice

Ringworm is not caused by a worm.

It's a fact!

Athlete's foot

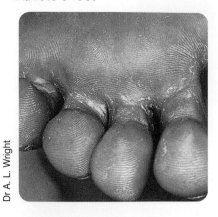

Dr A. L. Wright

Infectious condition that is found between the toes. It appears as small blisters which then burst. The skin can then become dry and itchy

- Services should not take place while the infection is present on the feet
- Refer for medical advice

Parasitic condition

scabies

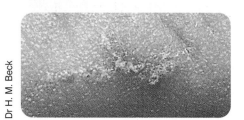

Dr H. M. Beck

A condition which is caused by the itch mite which burrows through the skin leaving greyish lines and reddish spots. The condition is extremely itchy particularly at night.

Is found in the folds of skin, which includes the hands and wrists

- Services should not take place while the infection is present
- Refer for medical advice

Other nail and skin conditions

There are certain conditions that, although don't prevent treatment, do restrict what can be offered. The nail treatment routine may have to be adapted.

CONDITION	CAUSE AND SYMPTOMS	TREATMENT
Ingrown nail Wellcome photo library	This is a painful condition where the nail grows into the side of the nail bed creating pressure and swelling. Most common on toenails, it can be caused by: - Cutting the nail too short and rounding off at the tip - Wearing shoes that are too small or too narrow, causing the nail to curl under and dig into the skin	- Treatments and services should not be carried out in the area affected

A bruised nail appears deep purple or black. In extreme cases the injury can result in the loss of the nail. A new nail will usually grow back again unless there is severe damage to the matrix.

It's a fact!

Bruised nail

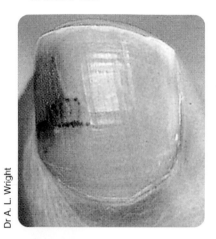

Dr A. L. Wright

- Damaging the toenail by stubbing the toes or dropping something on it
- Abnormal shaped nail bed

Caused by injury to the nail

- For mild bruising, avoid this part of the nail, and don't apply pressure
- If the whole nail is bruised it could be very painful. Don't treat the nail until it has healed

Pitting

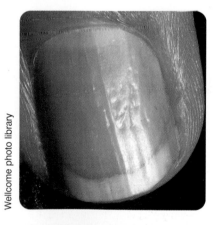

Wellcome photo library

Small pits on the surface of the nail plate, this can be caused by psoriasis or dermatitis

- Nail services can be carried out on the nail but you will need to work gently

Corns

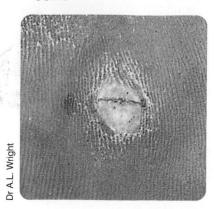

Dr A.L. Wright

Areas of hard skin usually found on the top or sides of the toe. They are caused by pressure from ill-fitting shoes

- Treatment should be sought from a chiropodist

It's a fact! White spots on the nail are not caused by a lack of calcium, it is usually the result of an injury, and the layers of the nail plate have separated in a small area

Nail biting

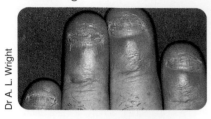

Dr A. L. Wright

Free edge is often very tender, and the cuticles may also be bitten

- A bitter-tasting product can be applied to the nails to discourage biting

Overgrown cuticles

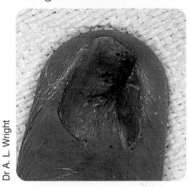

Dr A. L. Wright

The nail cuticle grows over the nail plate

- Lots of gentle cuticle work to loosen the cuticle, may take two or three manicures to see good results. Need to apply cuticle cream or oil each night

White spots on nail plate

Dr A. L. Wright

Can be as a result of an injury

- Avoid pressure over these areas. The white spots can be disguised by a coloured nail enamel

Ridges in nail plate

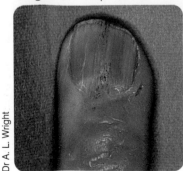

Dr A. L. Wright

Caused by illness, damage to the matrix, or old age

- Treat the nail gently and avoid too much pressure, as some nails may also be fragile

- Buffing can help reduce ridges, as can applying a ridge-filling base coat

Contra-actions

A **contra-action** is an unwanted reaction which occurs during or after a treatment.

Basic hand and nail treatment

A basic manicure treatment is carried out to improve the condition and appearance of the:

- **Lower arm**
- **Hands**
- **Cuticles**
- **Nails**

The lower arm

Sometimes, the skin of the lower arm can become dry due to neglect, sunburn or ageing. A body scrub can be used to **exfoliate** dead skin cells. Then the area needs to be moisturised by massaging cream or oil deep into the skin, especially around the elbow, which can be very dry

When you were a very young child, the skin of your hands would have been very smooth

iStockphoto.com/©Steven Derr

The hands

The hands are one of the first areas of the body to show the signs of ageing so it is important to look after them.

Hands are used constantly and get a lot of wear and tear – and it shows. The skin on the back of the hand can become very dry, rough, chapped, crepey and aged. The palms can become rough with **calluses**. The fingers can become cracked, which can be very sore.

A manicure will help to replace moisture to the skin of the hands, helping to keep them healthy, smooth and soft.

The cuticles

This is the area of skin around the base of the nail, which should be smooth, flexible and soft, with no breaks. However, if you do not look after your cuticles, they can become very dry, rough, tight and sometimes, spilt open. The aim of a manicure treatment is to restore moisture to the cuticle, so that the cuticle, once again, becomes soft and supple.

The appearance of the skin of hands changes with age

iStockphoto.com/© Robert Simon

The nails

Nails should be a healthy beige or pale pink colour. They should be flexible and have a smooth surface. The edge of the nail, known as the free edge, should be even and smooth.

It's a fact! Finger nails grow on average 0.5–1.2 mm per week. It can take approximately 4–6 months for a new nail to grow from the matrix to the free edge. Toenails grow more slowly.

It's a fact! A *pedicure* involves the care of the feet and toenails.

Preparing the treatment area for hand and nail services

When preparing your treatment area for hand or nail services you will need the following:

1 Manicure table or workstation, with chair

2 Towels

3 Comfortable chair

4 Washbasin

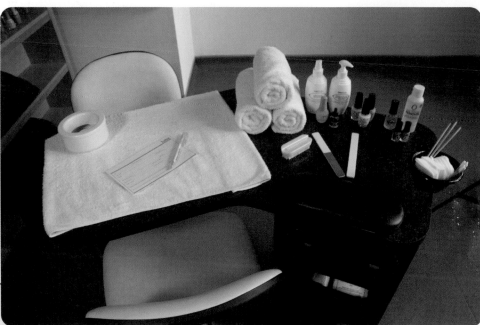

A prepared manicure table

© Habia

Equipment and materials

In order to be organised, efficient and professional, it is good practice to make sure you have all the equipment you need ready and prepared before you start a treatment.

Tools and equipment for the manicure station or table

TOOL/ EQUIPMENT	USE	BENEFITS	TIP
Nail files Courtesy of MAD Beauty	For shaping the free edge of the nail	Some files have a variety of surfaces, always end with the finest abrasive side to smooth the edge of the nail	The direction of filing should always be from the side to the centre, never in a sawing action across the free edge
Hoof stick Ellisons	To gently ease back the cuticle	As they are made from wood or plastic with a rubber end, they are better than using metal tools to loosen the cuticles	Use the rubber end and gently work in circles, to ease the skin at the base of the nail
Orange stick Ellisons	• Pointed end can clean under the free edge at the end of the treatment, to remove cream etc. • Can remove a small amount of product from a pot	The angled end can be covered with cotton wool and used like a hoof stick on the cuticle area	Use to clean up stray nail enamel, either dry or dipped in enamel remover
Nail scissors Ellisons	To reduce the length of longer nails, prior to filing	Can reduce nail length quickly, saving valuable time during the manicure. Scissors need to be large and strong enough to cut through thick nails	Never cut straight across, always angle the scissors, to avoid damaging the nail

Nail buffer  Courtesy of Creative Nail Design Inc. All CND products available from Sweet Squared	Promotes blood circulation to the nail and produces a shine on the nail surface	Improves health of the nail and smoothes the surface. Men often prefer a buffed 'natural shine' to the effect of clear enamel	Use fast strokes over the nail surface produce a smooth surface and a sheen and shine
High shine or three-way buffer  Courtesy of Creative Nail Design Inc. All CND products available from Sweet Squared	To smooth the nail and produce a sheen and shine	A three surface flexible buffer is much easier to use than a traditional buffer, often with better results	Always end with the finest abrasive side to get the best shine

Top tip A 'bevel' is a slanting edge, and if you file directly downwards over the free edge of the nail (bevelling) it can help to avoid the nail plate slitting and separating.

Digital Vision/Alamy

The manicure consultation

Consultation

When a professional nail technician prepares a client for a hand or nail treatment, they always carry out a consultation. This ensures it is safe to perform the treatment.

The consultation is the start of the relationship with a client.

During the consultation you need to find out information such as:

- Name
- Address
- Telephone number or mobile number
- Date of birth

Top tip You will have the chance to carry out a nail treatment as part of your Diploma course. Make sure that when you work with a client you are friendly, approachable and professional, so they are relaxed and at ease during the consultation process.

ACTIVITY

Plan a list of questions you would ask during the initial consultation for a manicure, and use these with a partner so you get used to asking questions and become more confident.

- Occupation
- Name of doctor
- Medical history (allergies, epilepsy, diabetes)
- Previous nail treatments
- Analysis of the condition of the hands, cuticles and nails

Record card

The **record card** is a very important document. One is completed at the initial consultation, and then updated after each visit.

It means there is a record of all the treatments provided, and of how the client reacted to the treatment. Records can also track any changes that have to be made during the treatment.

Hand and nail analysis

Before deciding on which nail treatments would be beneficial and what products to use, a professional nail technician will carry out a hand and nail analysis.

You will have the opportunity to do this as part of your Diploma course. You will need to look carefully at each area of the hands, cuticles and nails and record the results on a record card.

Treatment plan

As part of the consultation, after completing the analysis and client record card, a professional nail technician will complete a **treatment plan**.

You will have the opportunity to do this as part of your Diploma course. A treatment plan will enable you to focus on exactly what treatment is best, what products you will use and the expected outcome will be.

To avoid causing any harm when performing a manicure or spreading any infection it is very important to make sure you work hygienically and safely at all times.

Sterilising tools and equipment

A professional nail technician would never use dirty tools and equipment. They must be cleaned and sterilised before using them on clients. The methods for sterilising tools and equipments can be found in Chapter 2, first impressions count.

Top tip

A professional nail technician would show the client how to file their nails correctly, in case they needed to trim the free edge in between treatments.

ACTIVITY

Design and make a record card that you would want to use if you were offering nail treatments in a nail salon or spa. Use your record card with a partner to test it.

Find out if the record card needs improving.

Manicure products

Ellisons

Hand and nail care products

Once the condition of the hand and nails are known, products can be chosen.

The following list details the main hand and nail products used in manicures:

PRODUCT	APPLICATION	BENEFIT
Skin cleanser/ sanitiser	• Use to clean the hands before the hand treatment	• Removes harmful micro-organisms that could cause infection
Skin exfoliant	• Product designed to remove dead skin cells (exfoliate) • A cream containing fine particles that are abrasive and so slough off the dead skin cells • Used at the beginning of the manicure	• Removes dead skin cells • Prepares the skin for massage cream, which will be absorbed better • Leaves the skin smooth, soft and brighter
Nail enamel remover	• Usually contains acetone, and oil such as glycerol • Can dry the nail plate if used excessively • Applied on cotton wool pads	• Dissolves nail enamel and grease from the nail plate
Buffing paste	• Coarse texture, contains powdered pumice or silica • Very small amount needed • Used with a traditional buffer	• Smoothes the nail plate and gives a shine to the nail
Cuticle cream/oil	• Contains a mixture of fats, waxes and oil, e.g. beeswax, cocoa butter	• Replaces moisture • Softens and nourishes the cuticle, so it can be easily pushed back and loosened
Cuticle remover	• Contains potassium hydroxide, which is an alkaline and can be very drying on the nail • After cuticle work has been done ensure any excess is removed by gently using a nail brush	• Applied to the cuticles to help loosen it from the nail plate
Massage cream/oil	• Contains waxes, oils and perfumes • Used as a medium for the hand massage • Apply with hands, apply sufficient so the massage flows smoothly	• Replaces moisture, and leaves the hand soft and smooth

Base coat	• Apply one coat to a clean, grease-free nail plate	• Smooth base for the nail enamel • Prevents dark colours from staining the nail
Nail enamel	• Plain/cream nail enamel – apply 2 coats • Pearlised nail enamel – apply 3 coats (don't use a top coat)	
Top coat	• One coat applied on top of the nail enamel • Don't apply over pearlised nail enamel	• Adds extra gloss • Prolong life of the manicure/nail enamel • Protect nail enamel from chipping
Quick dry oil/spray	• Oil is drizzled over the top coat • A spray can be applied evenly	• Speeds up the drying process

Top tip

Nail enamel peels if:

- It is applied too thickly
- Poor quality or thickened nail enamel is used
- Oil or grease is left on the nail plate

Top tip

Nail enamel chips if:

- There are ridges on nail plate
- There is a flaking nail condition
- The nail enamel is dried too quickly
- The nail enamel has been thinned too much

Ellisons

Nail enamel remover can be available as a retail product for clients to use at home

Massage techniques

Massage strokes are classified into three main groups. Within each group there are a range of strokes. The table below lists the main movements in each of the three groups.

Top tip

Pearlised or chrystalline nail enamel is not recommended for dry nails

CLASSIFICATION/GROUP	INDIVIDUAL MOVEMENTS	MAIN USES AND EFFECTS
Effleurage (stroking) 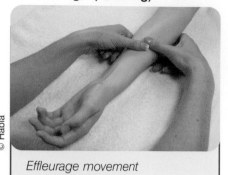 *Effleurage movement* © Habia	• Superficial effleurage • Deep effleurage • Stimulating stroking • Soothing stroking	• Increase blood circulation • Increases **lymphatic** circulation • Relieves tension • Helps reduce **non-medical oedema** • Aids **desquamation** • Help with relaxation
Petrissage (compression) 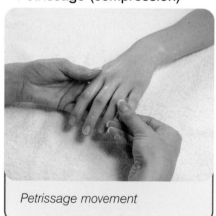 *Petrissage movement* © Habia	• Kneading • Knuckling • Skin rolling • Pinching • Wringing	• Increase blood circulation • Increases lymphatic circulation • Breaks down tight **nodules** in the muscles • Aids removal of waste products from the tissues • Promotes relaxation in the client
Tapotement (percussion) 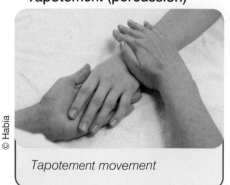 *Tapotement movement* © Habia	• Beating • Pounding • Hacking • Clapping/cupping	• Increases sluggish circulation • Stimulates the sensory nerve endings • Improves muscle tone and response • Stimulates a **lethargic** client

Nail treatment procedures

Now that you are aware of all the factors that affect the appearance and condition of the hands and nails, and you know how to select the right products and tools, and why you must carry out a consultation – you are ready to put the theory into practice!

EXTEND YOUR LEARNING
Research the international nail experts Marian Newman and Leighton Denny. Find out where they are based, what competitions they have won, about their own range of nail products and which celebrities are their clients … and learn just how far you can go in the nail industry.

Some people think that the massage is by far the best part of the manicure, it is so incredibly relaxing. So don't miss it out or rush it, as it may be disappointing for the client. They may feel that you have not given a full manicure treatment.

Top tip

Be careful not to use a 'sawing' action when filing the nails as this can cause the layers of the nail plate to split and separate.

Top tip

Try this site for Marian Newman http://www. showstudio.com/ contributors/326 Try this one for Leighton Denny http:/shop. helenmarks.co.uk/

Top tip

Step by step method for a manicure procedure

Carry out a consultation and fill in the record card. Analyse the hand and nails, and discuss the treatment plan

1 Cleanse the hands with an antiseptic spray to remove dirt and micro-organisms and remove nail enamel from both hands.

2 Start on the first hand, file the nails into a flattering shape.

3 Buff the nails lightly using the three-way buffer.

4 Apply cuticle oil to the cuticle area.

5 Massage cream/oil in gently.

6 Place hand in a bowl of warm water to soak. Meanwhile file nails on second hand, buff gently and apply cuticle cream.

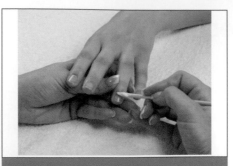

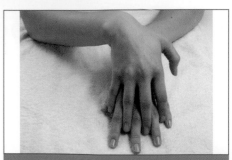

7 Remove first hand from bowl and dry with a towel, and place second hand in the warm water to soak.

8 Apply cuticle remover to the cuticles and with a 'tipped' orange stick, carefully push back the cuticles. Remove second hand from the bowl and thoroughly dry. Apply cuticle remover and carefully push back the cuticles with the orange stick.

9 Remove any excess cuticle remover with a damp nail brush and dry. Perform hand massage (see separate procedure). Hands are ready for the application of nail enamel, if appropriate (see different techniques).

Step by step method for a hand massage

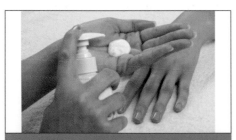

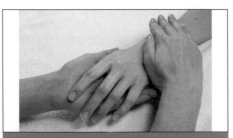

1 Apply sufficient massage cream/lotion in your palm and rub both hands together to spread the product evenly.

2 Using the palm apply three effleurage strokes to the outer part of the lower arm and hand, and then repeat to the inner part.

3 Use both thumbs in circular movements, work slowly from the elbow towards the wrist.

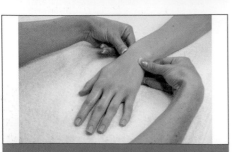

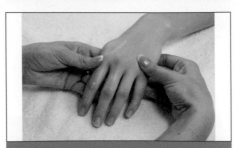

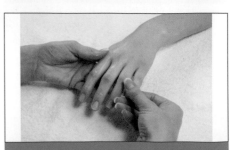

4 Carry out thumb kneading to the wrist area.

5 Carry out thumb kneading across the back of hands towards the fingers.

6 Apply thumb kneading to each finger.

7 Support the hand, start with the smallest finger and gently rotate each finger twice in each direction. Finish with a slight pull, and a sliding motion off the end of the finger.

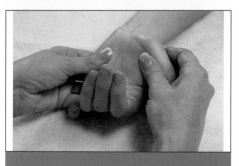

8 Turn the hand over; use your thumbs to apply deep circular kneading movements across the whole palm area, paying particular attention to the base of the thumb.

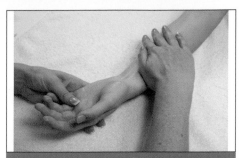

9 Finish with three effleurage strokes to each aspect of the lower arm and hand.

Bring your learning to life

When you are in the training salon or in your work placement, work with a partner and carry out a manicure treatment.

When you do this, you should ask your partner for feedback about the treatment.

When you have finished the service, write down your experiences in your Diploma file.

You should record:

- The condition of the hands and nails before the treatment.

- The products used for the treatment. Why did you choose them?

- The result – did it match the results identified in the treatment plan?

Then ask your partner to write in your Diploma file. They should write about their experience during the manicure treatment. How did the massage feel? What was the pressure like? Did they enjoy it?

Finally ask your partner what you could do to improve the manicure treatment next time. Note their answer. Then, when you carry out another manicure, refer back to your notes to see how you can improve.

It's a fact!

A professional manicure with enamel should take no more than 30 or 40 minutes. However, a file and enamel application can take as little as 10 minutes.

Top tip

Dark colours can draw attention to nails, so they are best avoided if the nails are very short, bitten or in a poor condition.

Step by step method for a manicure with transfer

Carry out the full manicure (see previous procedure) and discuss the desired final look and decide on the nail enamel colour.

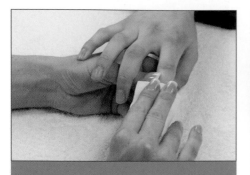

1 Remove any grease on the nail plate with the nail enamel remover.

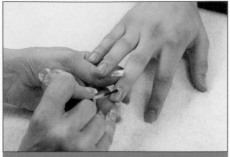

2 Select and apply the base coat.

3 Apply the first and second coat of enamel.

4 Tip an orange stick with cotton wool, wrap the cotton wool tightly around the orange stick, dip the tipped orange stick in enamel remover and remove any smudges of enamel, to ensure a perfect finish.

5 Select a nail transfer and soak it in water.

6 Use tweezers to slide the transfer from the backing paper.

7 Carefully apply the transfer to the nail, and ensure the transfer is positioned carefully on the nail.

8 Apply a coat of top coat/ sealer to protect the enamel, transfer and prolong the life of the manicure.

9 The final result can be very effective.

Bring your learning to life

When you are in the training salon or in your work placement, work with a **male** partner and carry out a manicure and transfer application.

When you do this, you should ask your partner for feedback about the treatment.

When you have finished the service, write down your experiences in your Diploma file.

You should record:

- The condition of the hands and nails before the treatment.

- The products used for the treatment. Why did you choose them? Which transfer did you choose?

- The result – did it match the results identified in the treatment plan?

Then ask your partner to write in your Diploma file. They should write about their experience during the manicure treatment. How did the massage feel? What was the pressure like? Did they enjoy it? Do they like the transfer?

Finally ask your partner what you could do to improve the manicure treatment and transfer application next time. Note their answer. Then, when you carry out another male manicure or transfer application, refer back to your notes to see how you can improve.

Correct nail enamel application

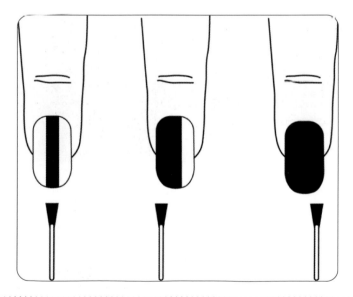

> **Top tip**
>
> A nail dryer speeds up the time it takes for the nail enamel to dry, which reduces smudges.

French manicure

The **French manicure** technique is designed to resemble a natural nail. The tips of the nail are painted white while the rest of the nail is enamelled in a pink, beige or other suitable shade.

> **It's a fact!**
>
> French manicures are thought to have originated in eighteenth-century Paris and were popular in the 1920s and 1930s.

Step by step method for a French manicure procedure

Carry out the full manicure (see previous procedure) and discuss the desired final look, then decide on the two colours to be used.

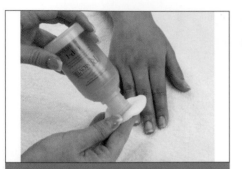

1 Remove nail enamel from both hands.

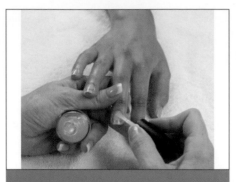

2 Select a base coat or appropriate strengthener and apply to the nails on both hands.

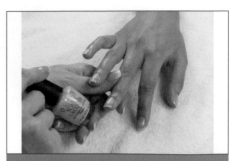

3 Select the most appropriate base colour – usually pale pink or beige.

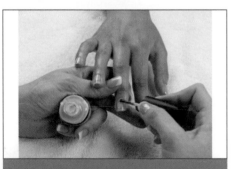

4 Apply the base colour.

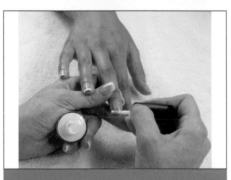

5 Apply the white tip to the free edge of the nails.

6 Apply a top coat/sealer to protect the nail enamel.

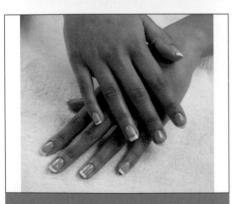

7 The final effect – groomed, natural-looking nails.

EXTEND YOUR LEARNING

 Research the different websites to find at least 10 different variations of French manicure. For example, look on the website

http://www.prom.net/nails to find out different styles.

Bring your learning to life

Creating the perfect 'smile line' is not easy - you need to have lots of practice. Record the improvements you make by taking photographs of your work. Take a photograph of your first attempt – even if it is not as good as you would have liked. Then, take another each time you have the opportunity to practice.

Arrange the photographs in a timeline to show the improvements you are making.

Here are some tips to help you:

- Don't paint the tip straight across the nail – create a 'smile'
- Ensure the whole of the nail tip is coloured and blended evenly
- Don't apply it too thick, as it will make a ridge and is more prone to chipping off
- Very opaque white can tend to be thicker and harder to apply expertly
- Make sure you take the white colour to the outer edges of the nail, in a sharp line, not rounded

Home care

Professional nail technicians always provide home care advice at the end of the treatments.

Treatment advice

Some clients may only visit a nail salon monthly, so it is important that the professional nail technician recommends products for them to use at home, to continue the effects of the treatment.

It's a fact!

There may be a small number of products that are only manufactured for use in a professional nail treatment procedure, and cannot be bought to be used at home.

All the products used in the salon should be available to buy for use at home

ACTIVITY

When you are in the training salon or on your work placement, investigate which hand and nail treatments are available. For example, manicure, pedicure, file/enamel, artificial nails. Then find out which are the most popular treatments.

You could also investigate what is the busiest time in the week for hand and nail treatments or which enamel colours are the most popular.

When you have finished your research, write a report about what you have found out and present your results to your group.

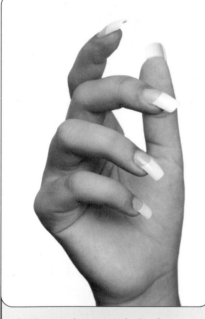

iStockphoto.com/parrus

Nails can be extended using a range of artificial nail systems

Technological developments

The nail industry is fast-paced and technology is constantly developing to support the needs of clients. Although many developments have been made in basic manicure treatments, it is with artificial nails that the most changes have been made over the past ten years.

Many different types of artificial nail products are available, but they are usually grouped into three systems:

- Acrylic
- UV gel
- Fibreglass

They all can produce excellent results as long as the nail technician is skilled and experienced.

The acrylic system was the first system to be developed commercially. The products used for this system are similar to those first used in the dental industry. The acrylic system is very popular in the UK and USA and involves mixing a liquid and a powder to form strong but flexible nails.

The UV gel system has also been developed from dental technology and involves a ready-mixed product that needs to be cured by ultraviolet light. As technology becomes more and more advanced, it appears to transfer very rapidly into the nail industry, producing more and more impressive, natural-looking nails.

The demand for artificial nails has increased greatly over the last few years, and new technology is helping to fuel the growth. The results are more natural, longer lasting and much more impressive.

The technology is constantly adapting, such as the use of the UV gel system to offer a 'permanent' nail enamel effect. A variety of colours and effects are available, including French manicure. People love the fact that their nail enamel lasts for weeks and weeks and never chips.

Technology in both nail systems and nail art is constantly pushing the boundaries, and this coupled with the strong link with the fashion industry makes this one of the most exciting industries to be part of.

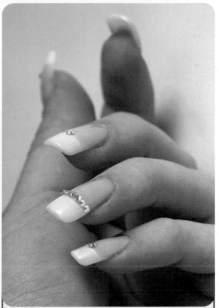

You can produce some fantastic results using artificial nail systems

iStockphoto.com/© Olga Vasilkova

EXTEND YOUR LEARNING

Artificial nail systems have had an enormous impact on the nail service industry. The technology of the products that are used has improved over time and the nails can look so natural that you can hardly tell the difference. Although some wear the extended nails so long that it is obvious that they are false – but that may be the wearers' intention!

There are now many different types of nail systems:

- Acrylic liquid and powder
- UV gel
- Nail tips
- Fibre

Investigate the different systems. Make a leaflet that would be available to clients explaining the benefits of each system.

What you have learnt

- Why the appearance of hands and nails is important:
    - Your hands and nails can say a great deal about your personality
    - Men have nail treatments too!
    - Your hands can reflect your health
- The structure of the nails and skin:
    - The nail unit is made up of three main parts – the nail bed, the matrix and the nail plate
    - The nails grow around 3.7 mm per month
    - The natural shape of the nail varies from one person to another
- The main factors affecting nail care services:
    - The factors that can affect hand and nail treatments must be considered before treatments take place

- Skin and nail conditions that affect services and treatments:

  - You cannot carry out hand and nail treatments if an infectious condition is present

- Basic hand care and nail treatments:

  - A basic hand and nail treatment is designed to improve the condition of the lower arm, hands, cuticles and nails

- How to prepare for hand and nail treatments:

  - Tools, equipment and materials need to be ready prior to the start of hand and nail treatments

  - A consultation must take place before the treatment is started

  - Hand and nail analysis allows you to plan the treatment

  - How to choose the correct products for the treatment

- How to carry out a basic hand and nail treatment:

  - There are three main massage movements used for hand and nail treatments – effleurage, petrissage and tapotement

  - The step by step methods for manicure treatments

  - The home care advice that should be given at the end of a hand and nail treatment

- The technological developments in nail services:

  - The developments in nail extension technology

Assessment activities

Crossword

Across

3 Another name more commonly used for the lunula (4, 4)

6 An example of a viral infection that can be found on fingers (4)

9 A condition found on the toe caused by wearing tight-fitting shoes (4)

11 The product that is painted on the nails to give them colour (4, 6)

13 The name of a person that carries out hand and nail treatments (4, 10)

14 This can be reflected in your hands and nails (9)

16 The part of the nail that grows beyond the finger tip (4, 4)

Down

1 This condition is not really a worm (4, 4)

2 This is carried out before a nail treatment begins (12)

4 A very natural look, popular with brides (6, 8)

5 A very relaxing part of a manicure treatment (7)

7 The results of a consultation are recorded on this (6, 4)

8 Nails are _____ at the end of a manicure treatment to make them shine (6)

10 Used for shaping the free edge of the nail (4)

12 The nail plate sits on this (4, 3)

15 Where an ingrown nail is most likely to be found (3)

Wordsearch

```
N M K Z X Q E A R D S Q U A R E R J G
A W R I S T E L Q E P O N Y C H I U M
I C C O N T R A I N D I C A T I O N K
C W C E W K Z E F F L E U R A G E Q A
I B Z M W G T V P Q G G D M T G E G F
N Y R F E E N T N E M E T O P A T M O
H C C U H O R I J B T O E E U Q A A N
C C O A I E V W R U A R R M Q V Z T Y
E F N B F S A A J F N U I M M N U R C
T D S F D R E G L F C C F S A I J I H
S S U P T S I S C I S S O R S T L X O
E B L N S W W D N N S A R U S A D I L
I C T E A Z Y A G G E O F W A R G H Y
B U A K F I M Q I E U N Z P G E P E S
A T T A H I L G I N O T A Z E K W Q I
C I I L B L N K D H V H J M F T Z V S
S C O F O Q L G R O W T H H E G B G L
J L N S L S O P E X M K B I F L E I H
V E R R U C A G Q R X W F B U N X O Y
```

Bruise	File	Massage	Scissors
Bufffer	Finger	Matrix	Square
Buffing	Fingers	Nail	Squoval
Consultation	Flake	Onycholysis	Tapotement
Contraindication	Grow	Oval	Technician
Cuticle	Growth	Petrissage	Verruca
Effleurage	Hands	Ridge	Wart
Enamel	Hangnail	Ringworm	Wrist
Eponychium	Keratin	Round	
File	Manicure	Scabies	

Multiple choice questions

1 A manicure involves the care of:
   a the hands and fingernails
   b the nails and toes
   c the feet and toenails
   d the hands and feet

2 Men are likely to choose this after a manicure treatment:
   a pale pink enamel
   b buffing
   c filing
   d white enamel

3 Someone who works in the nail industry is known as a:
   a beauty therapist
   b spa therapist
   c hairdresser
   d nail technician

4 The nail bed is the place where this sits:
   a the matrix
   b the free edge
   c the nail plate
   d the nail length

5 The matrix:
   a is where the nail bed is formed
   b is where the nail cuticle is formed
   c is where the nail edge is formed
   d is where the nail plate is formed

6 The curve at the bottom of the nail plate is known as the:

   a the lunula

   b the luna

   c the lunar

   d the linula

7 The section of the nail plate that extends past the bed is called:

   a the edge

   b the length

   c the free edge

   d the nail tip

8 The average rate that a nail grows in an adult is about:

   a 3.7 cm per month

   b 0.37 mm per month

   c 37 mm per month

   d 3.7 mm per month

9 If the skin of the hands is dehydrated, it means they are:

   a hydrated

   b dry

   c wet

   d cold

10 Moisturising the skin of the hands will keep it:

   a in poor condition

   b in good condition

   c damp

   d wet

Label the diagram

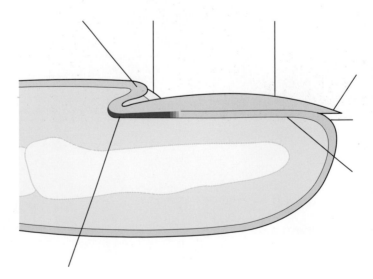

Answer section

Assessment activities for Chapter 1

Crossword

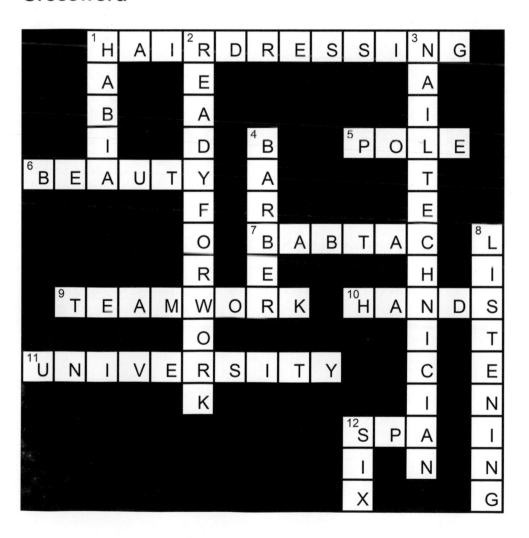

Wordsearch

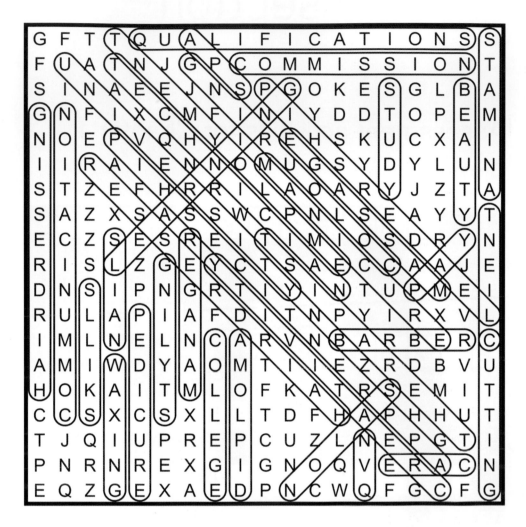

Multiple choice questions

1 The number of separate industries for hair and beauty is:

   a six

   b four

   c three

   d seven

2 A barber:

   a colours hair

   b cuts the hair of women

   c styles hair

   d cuts the hair of men and boys

3 Someone who does nail art is a:

   a beauty therapist

   b spa therapist

   c hairdresser

   d nail technician

4 The Diploma in Hair and Beauty Studies is a:

  a ready for work qualification

  b **preparation for work qualification**

  c preparation for hairdressing qualification

  d qualification for beauty therapy

5 Teamwork in the hair and beauty industries is important because:

  a working as a team keeps the salon clean

  b working as a team means you get the chance to talk to your friends at work

  c working as a team means everyone likes each other

  d **working as a team helps the business run smoothly**

6 NVQ Level 1 is a qualification for:

  a **assisting in the salon**

  b hairdressing in the salon

  c beauty therapy

  d nail services

7 A competence-based qualification:

  a prepares you for work

  b prepares you for exams

  c makes sure you are ready for study

  d **makes sure you are ready for work**

8 Someone who carries out a waxing treatment is most likely to be known as a:

  a nail technician

  b hairdresser

  c **beauty therapist**

  d spa therapist

9 To work at a management level in the hair and beauty industries you need to have:

  a an NVQ level 3

  b advanced diploma in hair and beauty studies

  c **foundation degree**

  d vocational qualification

10 ANT is an organisation for:

  a hairdressers

  b **nail technicians**

  c spa therapists

  d barbers

Match the service with the job role

Draw an arrow to the person most likely to carry out the hair or beauty service

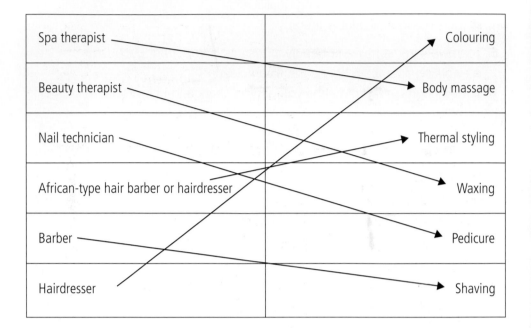

Assessment activities for Chapter 2

Crossword

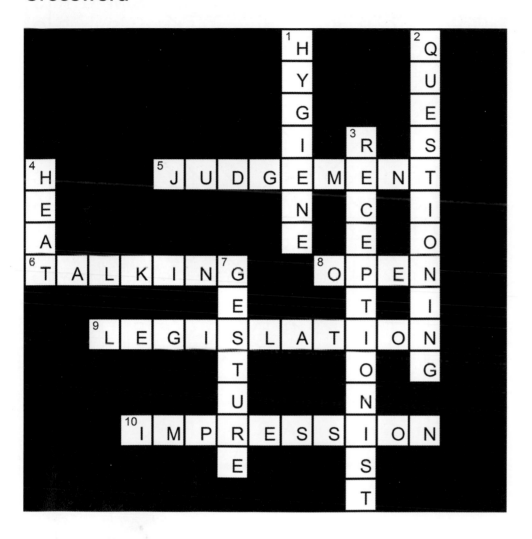

Wordsearch

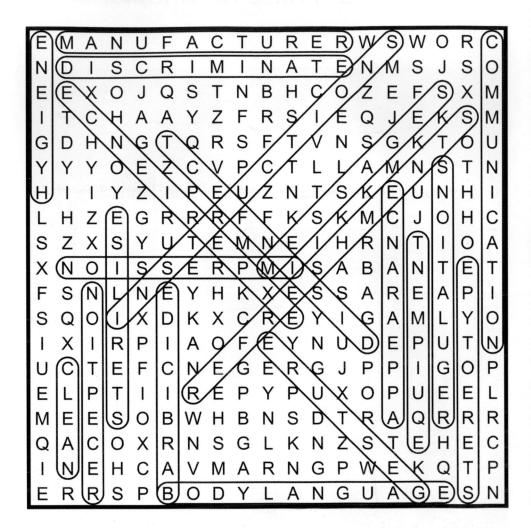

```
E M A N U F A C T U R E R W S W O R C
N D I S C R I M I N A T E N M S J S O
E E X O J Q S T N B H C O Z E F S X M
I T C H A A Y Z F R S I E Q J E K S M
G D H N G T Q R S F T V N S G K T O U
Y Y Y O E Z C V P C T L L A M N S T N
H I I Y Z I P E U Z N T S K E U N H I
L H Z E G R R F F K S K M C J O H C
S Z X S Y U T E M N E I H R N T I A
X N O I S S E R P M I S A B A N T T
F S N L N E Y H K X E S S A R E M P I
S Q O I X D K X C R E Y I G A M L Y O
I X I R P I A O F E Y N U D E P U T N
U C T E F C N E G E R G J P P I G O P
E L P T I R E P Y P U X O P U E R L R
M E E S O B W H B N S D T R A Q R E C
Q A C O X R N S G L K N Z S T E H E P
I N E H C A V M A R N G P W E K Q T P
E R R S P B O D Y L A N G U A G E S N
```

Assessment activities for Chapter 3

Crossword

Wordsearch

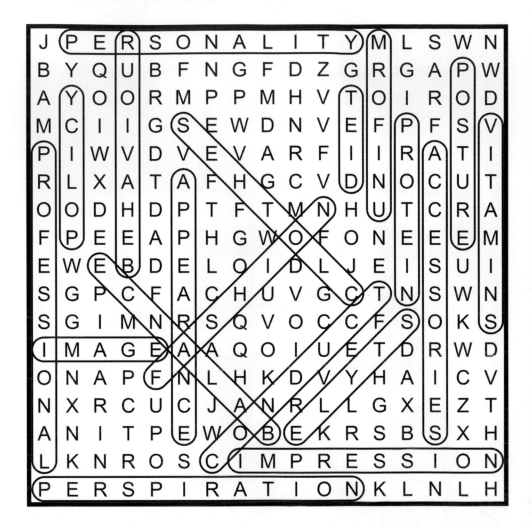

```
J P E R S O N A L I T Y M L S W N
B Y Q U B F N G F D Z G R G A P W
A Y O O R M P P M H V T O I R O D
M C I I G S E W D N V E F P F S V
P I W V D V E V A R F I I R A T I
R L X A T A F H G C V D N O C U T
O O D H D P T F T M N H U T C R A
F P E E A P H G W O F O N E E M I
E W E B D E L O I D L J E I S U N
S G P C F A C H U V G C T N S W S
S G I M N R S Q V O C C F S O K D
I M A G E A A Q O I U E T D R W V
O N A P F N L H K D V Y H A I C V
N X R C U C J A N R L L G X E Z T
A N I T P E W O B E K R S B S X H
L K N R O S C I M P R E S S I O N
P E R S P I R A T I O N K L N L H
```

Foods and food groups

Identify the type of food in the left-hand column and write down in the right-hand column the food group or groups that it supplies.

TYPE OF FOOD	FOOD GROUP
	Fibre, vitamins, mineral salts

Proteins, saturated fat, vitamins, mineral salts

Proteins, saturated fat, vitamins, mineral salts

Proteins, saturated fat

Carbohydrates, fibre

Trans fats

Mineral salts, fibre, vitamins

iStockphoto.com/© Naomi Bassitt

Carbohydrates, fibre

iStockphoto.com/Floortje

Vitamins, proteins, mineral salts

Assessment activities for Chapter 4

Crossword

Wordsearch

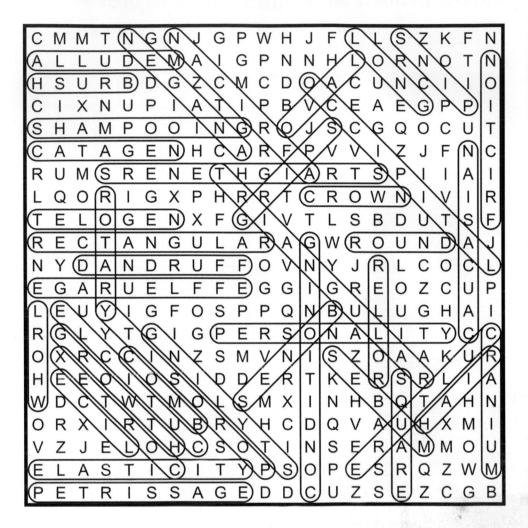

Match the statements

Hair grows and then falls out in a continuous cycle. Match the statements to the correct stage of the hair growth cycle by drawing an arrow from one to the other.

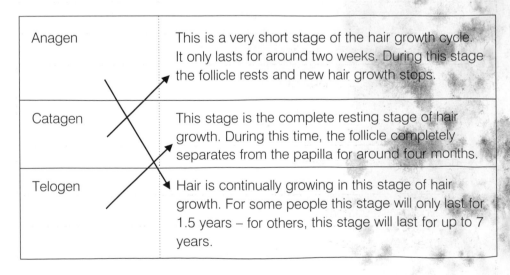

Anagen	This is a very short stage of the hair growth cycle. It only lasts for around two weeks. During this stage the follicle rests and new hair growth stops.
Catagen	This stage is the complete resting stage of hair growth. During this time, the follicle completely separates from the papilla for around four months.
Telogen	Hair is continually growing in this stage of hair growth. For some people this stage will only last for 1.5 years – for others, this stage will last for up to 7 years.

Colour in the bones

Illustration of the cranium with frontal, parietal and occipital bones labelled

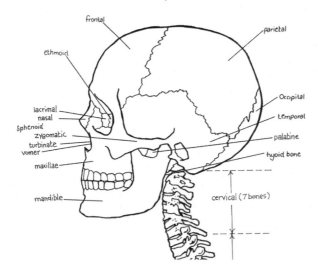

frontal

parietal

ethmoid

Occipital

temporal

lacrimal
nasal
Sphenoid
zygomatic
turbinate
vomer

palatine

hyoid bone

maxillae

mandible

cervical (7 bones)

True or False
Answer

	TRUE	FALSE
Terminal hair is soft and downy and found on the faces of women		✓
Hair in good condition will have a smooth cuticle	✓	
A porosity test is used to find out the condition of the cuticle	✓	
All hairs have a medulla		✓
Sebum is the natural oil of the hair	✓	
A cowlick is found at the nape of the neck		✓
Head lice are a parasite	✓	
The hair has a muscle called the arrector pili	✓	
African-type hair is straight		✓
Hair texture is the diameter of a single strand of hair	✓	

Assessment activities for Chapter 5

Crossword

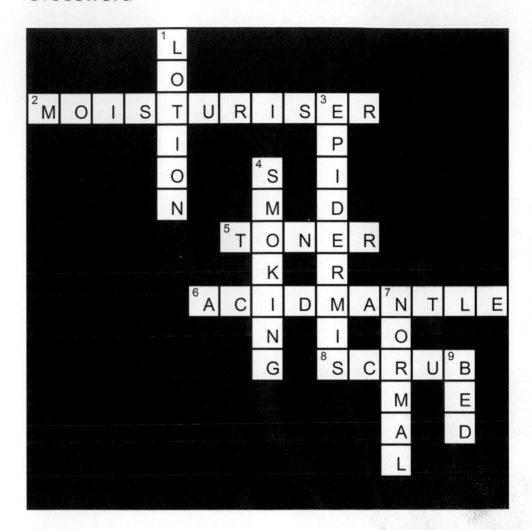

Wordsearch

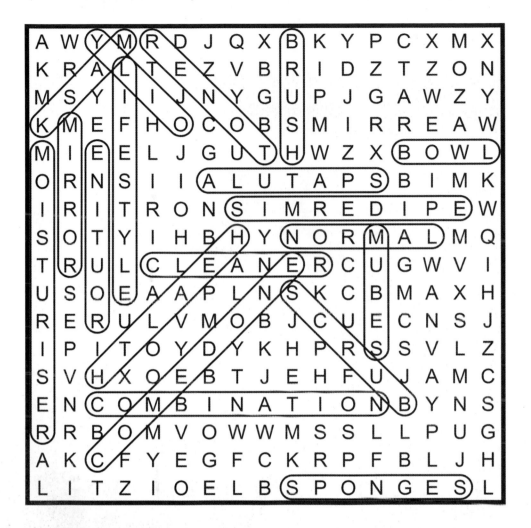

The five layers of the epidermis

Label the diagram.

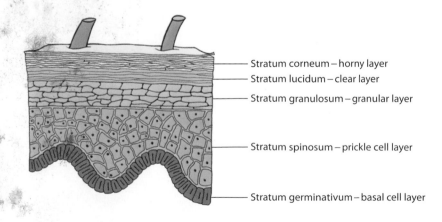

Stratum corneum – horny layer
Stratum lucidum – clear layer
Stratum granulosum – granular layer
Stratum spinosum – prickle cell layer
Stratum germinativum – basal cell layer

Cross-section of the skin

Label the diagram.

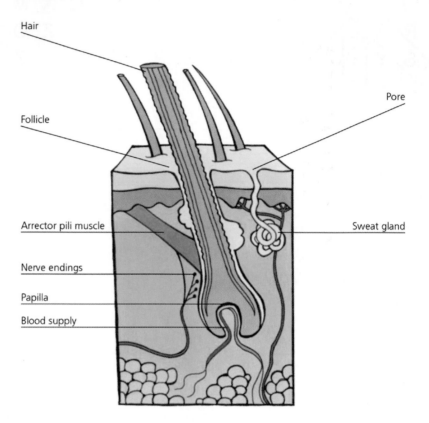

Hair

Pore

Follicle

Arrector pili muscle

Sweat gland

Nerve endings

Papilla

Blood supply

Skin types

Link the skin types on the left with the skin characteristics on the right. You may use different coloured markers to show your connections.

Skin types

Skin characteristics

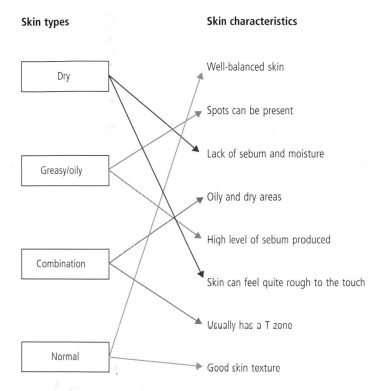

Dry

Greasy/oily

Combination

Normal

Well-balanced skin

Spots can be present

Lack of sebum and moisture

Oily and dry areas

High level of sebum produced

Skin can feel quite rough to the touch

Usually has a T zone

Good skin texture

Assessment activities for Chapter 6

Crossword

Wordsearch

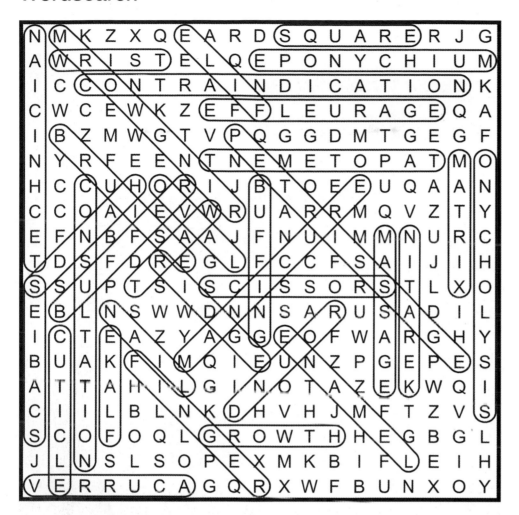

Multiple choice questions

1 A manicure involves the care of:

   a **the hands and fingernails**

   b the nails and toes

   c the feet and toenails

   d the hands and feet

2 Men are likely to choose this after a manicure treatment:

   a pale pink enamel

   b **buffing**

   c filing

   d white enamel

3 Someone who works in the nail industry is known as a:

   a beauty therapist

   b spa therapist

   c hairdresser

   d **nail technician**

4 The nail bed is the place where this sits:

   a the matrix

   b the free edge

   c the nail plate

   d the nail length

5 The matrix:

   a is where the nail bed is formed

   b is where the nail cuticle is formed

   c is where the nail edge is formed

   d is where the nail plate is formed

6 The curve at the bottom of the nail plate is known as the:

   a the lunula

   b the luna

   c the lunar

   d the linula

7 The section of the nail plate that extends past the bed is called:

   a the edge

   b the length

   c the free edge

   d the nail tip

8 The average rate that a nail grows in an adult is about :

   a 3.7 cm per month

   b 0.37 mm per month

   c 37 mm per month

   d 3.7 mm per month

9 If the skin of the hands is dehydrated, it means they are:

   a hydrated

   b dry

   c wet

   d cold

10 Moisturising the skin of the hands will keep it:

   a in poor condition

   b in good condition

   c damp

   d wet

Label the diagram

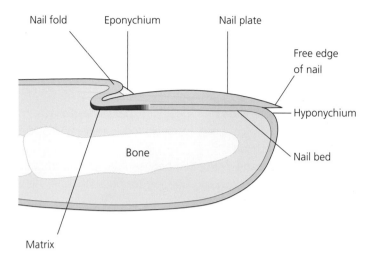

Nail fold   Eponychium   Nail plate

Free edge
of nail

Hyponychium

Bone

Nail bed

Matrix

Glossary

absorption take into the body through the skin

acid mantle slightly acidic film on the surfacce of the skin that protects it against bacteria, etc.

afro hair style which accentuated the curliness of African type hair

airbrushing painting technique where paint is blown by compressed air on to the surface to be coated

alabaster white, translucent form of gypsum, often carved into ornaments

alcohol in skin toners, provides a cooling effect

allergic reaction adverse reaction of the body to products or substances

alopecia hair loss: **alopecia areata** hair loss occurs in circular or oval patches, if the bald patches join together the condition is known as **alopecia totalis**, hair loss over the whole of the scalp; **cicatricial alopecia** is caused by damage to the dermis; **traction alopecia** caused by excessive tension on the hair

alpha keratin see **keratin**

aluminium pigment used in makeup, gives a metallic effect

amino acids constituent of protein

ammonium hydroxide lifts and opens the cuticle in nail treatments; speeds up bleaching process of hydrogen peroxide in hair treatments

ammonium thioglycollate chemical compound used in hair **perming** to break the **disulphide bridges**

anarchy a state of lawlessness

androgynous having the characteristics of both sexes

antibodies produced by the body to fight infection and carried by the **lymphatic system**

apocrine glands sweat gland located in the arm pits, nipples and groin excreting a fluid that contains **pheromones**; activity of these glands is increased by stress or excitement

arrector pili muscle muscle connected to the base of the hair follicle that causes the hair to either lie flat against the skin or stand at right angles to it

assimilation the process of becoming like the surrounding population in order to fit in to the existing system

astringent strong form of skin toner, can be drying to the skin

atoms smallest particle of a chemical element

autoclave machine that uses pressurised steam to sterilise metal tools

azo dyes acid dyes found in temporary colours; give bright intense colour

bactericidal, bactericides substances that kill bacteria

barbicide™ chemical used to clean tools; they will not be completely sterilised

basement membrane structure between the epithelium and connective tissue providing support to the epithelium; also known as the hypodermis

bed epithelium thin layer of tissue attaching the nail plate to the nail bed

beta keratin see **keratin**

black identity social grouping for people of African descent, particularly those descended from peoples forcibly removed from Africa during the sixteenth to nineteenth centuries as a result of the slave trade

blood vessels tube-like structures that carry blood around the body: arteries carry oxygenated blood pumped from the lungs by the heart; veins carry deoxygenated blood back

body language ways of deliberately or subconsciously expressing our thoughts, feelings, wishes by our body position, facial expressions, etc.

Body Mass Index (BMI) a statistical measurement comparing a person's weight to their height. It is calculated by dividing weight in kilograms by the square of height in metres

body odour unpleasant smell caused by stale sweat being left on the body

bone marrow substance found within the hollow interior of the bones; red bone marrow produces new blood cells and yellow bone marrow is used as a storage area for fat cells

bones the hard structures that makes up the basic framework of the **skeleton**

bulb base of the root of the hair containing the cells that divide to become a hair

buying signals **body language** of someone who is about to decide to buy a product or service

calcium metallic element found in bones, giving them strength

callus thickened area of skin, frequently caused by friction

capillaries small blood vessels, carrying blood to the extremities of the organs

carbohydrates energy-producing element of our food, found in starch, sugar, glucose

carbon non-metallic element, used, probably in the form of graphite or charcoal, by the Ancient Egyptians to make a black dye for makeup

cartilage firm, elastic connective tissue; **elastic cartilage** extremely flexible form of cartilage used to form, for example, the ear; **fibrocartilage** tougher and less flexible than hyaline cartilage, it forms pads between bones as, for example, in the spine; **hyaline cartilage** covers the ends of bones where they meet and prevents friction

cationic having a positive electric charge

cavity space

cell the smallest element of organic structures

census government questionnaire, conducted every ten years to gather demographic information on the total population

cerussite a white carbonate of lead used by the Ancient Egyptians to lighten black kohl eye makeup; now known to be poisonous

chemotherapy chemical treatment, most often associated with cancer

cheque guarantee card card issued by banks to indicate they will honour a personal chaeque up to a certain amount

cicatricial alopecia *see* **alopecia**

circuit continuous path of an electrical current

clinical waste any waste products that may be contaminated with bodily fluids

closed questions questions that can only be answered by 'yes' or 'no'

code of practice set of rules to ensure safe and consistent working across all workplaces

collagen protein found in bones, giving them resilience

collagen fibres fibres in the skin that give it strength

colour circle method of illustrating the inter-relationships of colours: if the circle is divided into six radiating segments, the primary colours sit in alternate segments, with the secondary colours in between: orange between yellow and red, purple between red and blue, and green between blue and yellow; colours directly opposite each other are known as complimentary colours: red is opposite green, yellow is opposite purple and blue is opposite orange; in hair colouring, complimentary colours can neutralise each other

colour spectrum the seven colours we see as a rainbow: red, orange, yellow, green, blue, indigo and violet

commission a proportional sum of money paid to someone who sells a service or product

competence based assessment method measured by considering a person's ability to undertake certain tasks

competitors other people or organisations offering the same services and products as you

conditioning agents help to protect the hair and provide softness and shine

conduction transmission of heat or electricity by contact

conductor substance that allows electricity to pass through it easily

consultation conversation between therapist and client prior to treatment to establish certain facts about the client and the treatment, and discuss the desired outcomes

Continuing Professional Development (CPD) programme designed to continue training in a chosen profession

contra-action action taken to avoid an unwanted reaction to a treatment

contra-indication any condition that will prevent a treatment being carried out

convection transmission of heat or electricity without physical contact, i.e. through the air

cornrows hair style, originally of West African origin, that consists of tiny plaits laid in rows close to the head

cortex main section of the hair

cortical cells the cells that make up the **cortex** of the hair

cosmetologist a US term for someone who carries out both hair and beauty treatments

cranium eight bones that enclose the brain

credit card when someone pays using a credit card, the amount is not taken from their bank account immediately; they receive a monthly bill for all the transactions they have made in that period; *see* **debit card**

cross infection passing infection from one area of the body or one person to another

curl development test used to assess the progress of a perming treatment

cutiolo layer of dead tissue around the edge of the nail plate that seals the space between the skin and the nail plate

dandruff dead skin cells forming on the scalp

debit card when someone pays using a debit card, the amount is taken from their bank account immediately; *see* **credit card**

depth how light or dark a colour is

dermis inner layer of skin

design brief an instruction detailing what is required

designated person an individual who has the appropriate qualifications and skills to take charge in certain situations, e.g. there may be a designated First Aider

desquamation removal of dead skin cells

detergent cleansing agent

disinfected cleansed

disposable income the amount of money a person has to spend after they have paid for essentials such as accommodation, food and transport

disulphide bridges a link holding two sulphur atoms together; in the hair cross links between **polypeptide chains**; **perming** breaks and reforms **disulphide bridges**

dreadlocks locked coils of hair; can form naturally if hair is uncombed for long periods or can be formed deliberately; often associated with Rastafarians; also known as *locks* or *dreads*

dreads   *see* **dreadlocks**

dyslexia   disability whereby sufferers find it difficult to interpret the written word while their understanding of the spoken word is unimpaired; also known as word blindness

eccrine glands   sweat-producing glands

elastic cartilage   *see* **cartilage**

elasticity test   indicates the hair's condition - if it can be stretched and will naturally return to its normal length, this indicates that the cortext is undamaged and the hair is in good condition

electron   elementary particle with negative electrical charge

employability skills   those skills that are relevant for many industries

enamel/polish secure   any of a range of items designed to be placed on wet **nail enamel** and kept in place by a coat of sealant: includes beads, rhinestones, foil shapes, metal studs, etc.

epidermis   outer layer of skin

eponychium   living skin at the base of the nail plate covering the matrix area

ethics   morally correct behaviour; knowing the difference between right and wrong, especially in our dealings with other people

eumelanin   type of melanin that creates black and brown colour

exfoliate   remove dead cells from the skin's surface

fades   haircutting technique used to create a close-cropped hairstyle

faradic   form of electrical stimulation using alternating current with pulse widths of less than 1 ms to induce muscle contraction

fats   constituent of our food, found in meat, dairy products, chocolate, snack foods; while some is essential, too much is dangerous

fibre   grainy or threadlike element of food, found mainly in fruit and vegetables and essential for the proper functioning of our bodies

fibroblasts   cells which make up the protein and collagen fibres in the skin

fibrocartilage   *see* **cartilage**

fibula   bone of the lower leg

flotation   spa treatment to aid relaxation; the client floats in a special chamber

franchise   authorisation to sell a company's goods or services; a form of licence

franchisee   someone who buys a franchise

frankincense   aromatic gum resin from trees of the genus *Boswelia*, burnt as incense

free edge   the section of the nail plate that extends beyond the nail bed

freehand   done without artifical aid

freelance   someone who does not have one employer, but may undertake tasks for a number of clients

French manicure   method of painting fingernails where the tip is white and the rest of the nail is pink or beige

fungicidal, fungicides   substance that kills fungus

galvanic   form of electrical stimulation utilising interrupted direct current with pulsewidths of about 100 ms; induces muscle contraction

general waste   any waste products that are not contaminated with bodily fluids

genetic inheritance   what is passed down to you from your parents and grandparents through your genes, for example, hair colour and type

global   relating to the whole world

granite   naturally occuring mineral that gives water its taste, especially in soft water areas

gross price   the total price including tax; *see* **net price**

hair follicle   part of the skin that grows a hair

hard water   water containing a quantity of dissolved minerals such as **calcium** or **magnesium**

hazard   something that has the potential to cause harm

henna   a tropical shrub. The roots and leaves are dried, ground and mixed with, e.g. citrus juice to produce a paste that can be used to colour and condition the hair

hieroglyph   symbol for a letter or sound, as used in Ancient Egyptian and other writing

high frequency   3–30 megahertz

hormones   secreted by certain organs in the body to stimulate other organs to action

hot comb   thermal equipment used to straighten African type hair

humectants   in skin toners, keep the moisture in the upper layer of the epidermis

hyaline cartilage   *see* **cartilage**

hydrogen bonds   links holding bundles of macrofibrils together – can be broken by water; *see* **salt linkages**, **sulphur bonds**

hydrogen peroxide   an oxidising agent used in hairdressing services when colouring or neutralising perms or relaxers. Also used within beauty treatments when tinting eyelashes and eyebrows

hydrogen peroxide   weak acid used to bleach the hair

hydrophilic   attracts water

hydrophobic   attracts oil

hydrotherapy   use of water based treatments to ease pain and for certain diseases

hygiene   principles and practice of maintaining health and cleanliness

hygroscopic   absorbs moisture

hypodermis   *see* **basement membrane**

hyponychium   slightly thickened layer of skin that lies underneath the free edge of the nail plate to create a seal to prevent micro-organisms infecting the nail bed

image   idea of how one should look, including hair, clothing, makeup

incineration   method of **waste management** whereby it is burned

incompatibility test   designed to check whether the hair has previously been treated with metallic salts

Individual Learning Plan   a progression for learning designed to suit one person

ingestion   take into the body by swallowing

inhalation   take into the body by breathing

insulator   substance that does not allow electricity to pass through it

International Colour Chart (ICC)   chart developed to standardise hair colours to ensure that the results of an application by a hairdresser can be reliably predicted

ion exchange   process of softening water by removing calcium and magnesium and replacing them with sodium

jacuzzi   bath which has air jets in the sides, creating bubbles and streams in the water

keratin   protein in the skin that makes it tough and prevents substances passing through it; **alpha keratin** form of the keratin when hair is in its natural state; **beta keratin** form of the keratin when has been stretched and dried

keratinisation   process whereby cells harden into **keratin**

keratinocyte   cell that produces **keratin**

kohl   a powder, usually antimony sulphide or lead sulphide, used in eye makeup

landfill   method of **waste management** whereby it is buried

langerhan cells   cells in the prickle cell layer of the skin that absorb and remove foreign bodies

lanolin   used as a conditioner and helps to remove colour

laser hair removal   method of removing unwanted hair using specialist laser equipment that passes laser energy through the skin to stop the hair from growing

laurionite   a white mineral compound of basic lead chloride

learner centred   educational programme designed around the learner's needs

legislation   the laws passed by Parliament

lethargic   feeling of tiredness and lacking in energy

liberty spikes   hairstyle where the hair is worn in a number of spikes standing at right angles to the head, inspired by the Statue of Liberty

ligament   short band of strong tissue holding bones together

lithium hydroxide   ingredient of relaxing hair treatment

local authority   body which has responsibility for community policies on business, education, environment and planning, fire and public safety, health and social care, leisure and transport

locks   see **dreadlocks**

lunula   part of the matrix of the nail that can be seen at the base of the nail plate; also known as the half moon

lymphatic system   network of conduits carrying lymph around the body, transporting fatty acids to the circulatory system and antigen presenting cells when an immune response is stimulated

macrofibrils   bundles of elongated cells, twisted together to form the **cortex** of the hair

magnesium   naturally occurring mineral that gives water its taste, especially in hard water areas

malachite   bright green mineral used by the Ancient Egyptians to make a green dye for makeup

mandible   jaw bone

manganese   a black mineral used by the Ancient Egyptians to make a black dye for makeup

manicure   cosmetic treatment of hands and fingernails

marketing plan   schedule drawn up to initiate or improve the sales of a product or service

medulla   spongy cells creating a space within the central core of a hair; fine hair tends not to have a medulla

(mehndi)   application of henna to feet, hands and nails

melanin   skin pigment that determines the colour of the skin, hair and eyes

melanocyte cell   cell that produces melanin

mesdemet   black eye makeup made by the Ancient Egyptians from galena, a lead ore

metacarpals   five bones that make up the hand

metatarsal   five bones that make up the foot

micro-business   a small business, generally having fewer than five employees

microcurrent   extremely low electrical current measured in millionths of an amp; used in treatments to stimulate cell growth, renewal and healing

microfibrils   small bundles of cells which join together to create **macrofibrils**

micron   one millionth of a metre

micro-organisms   very tiny organism that cannot be seen with the naked eye; includes bacteria, fungi, viruses, etc.

migrate   to move to another area or country

mineral salts   any of a number of elements present in many foodstuffs and essential to normal growth and functioning

mohawk   hairstyle where the hair stands vertically from the scalp in a fanned narrow strip from the hairline to the nape of the neck; the sides are shaved or very short

multi-task perform more than one task at once

myrrh aromatic gum resin from trees of the genus *Commiphora*, used in perfumery and medicine and burnt as incense

mytosis process whereby cells divide

nail art form of nail decoration using enamels, paints, transfers, jewels, glitter, etc.

nail enamel coloured paint designed for fingernails

nail enamel remover solvent used to take nail varnish off nails

nail technician a person who performs manicures and nail art

National Occupational Standards (NOC) government standards designed to raise people's business skills to a nationally recognised level

National Vocational Qualification (NVQs) work related, **competence based**, nationally recognised qualifications

nerves fibres or bundles of fibres carrying impulses between the brain and all areas of the body

net price the price excluding tax; *see* **gross price**

neurons element of the peripheral nervous system that send messages to the central nervous system

neutralising the part of the **perming** process where new **disulphide bridges** are formed

New Kingdom period in Ancient Egypt judged to be from 1550 to 1069 BC

nito dyes found in semi permanent colour, the colours are made alkaline to help them penetrate the hair cuticle.

nodule small rounded lump in the muscles caused by tightness or swelling

non-medical oedema build-up of fluid that does not have a medical cause

non-verbal communication any form of communication that does not use words: waving, pointing, facial expressions, etc.

norm a pattern of behaviour, attitude or values that is specific to a group or subculture

nucleus central part (of a cell)

nutrients substances used to provide nourishment, for example foods which fuel the body and give us energy

occupational asthma respiratory disease brought on by exposure to dust or fumes at work

ochre mineral of clay used to make a range of pigments from light yellow to brown or red to colour makeup

Old Kingdom period in Ancient Egypt judged to be from 3100 to 2125 BC

open questions questions that prompt someone to give information; usually begin with 'what', 'who', 'where', 'when', 'would', or 'how'

ossification hardening of the bones with age

osteoclasts cells that break down old bone cells and form new bone cells

osteocytes mature osteoclasts

overheads the routine costs for operating a business which are not directly related to a particular activity within the business, but are necessary for the business to function

papillae on the surface of the skin, tiny projections containing nerve endings and capillaries

papillary outer layer of the dermis

para dyes found in quasi and permanent colour

para-phenylenediamines (PPD) a chemical substance used in permanent oxidation hair colours

parasite animal or plant living in or on another and getting all its nutrient from it

patterns haircutting technique used to create lines and curves in the hair, creating a design or image within a haircut

pearlescent pigment used in makeup, adds an impression of transparency

peptides chain of amino acids

permanent colour hair colour that cannot be washed out and has to grow out

perming hair treatment that creates curls or waves and lasts until the hair grows out

personal protective equipment (PPE) clothing and equipment such as gloves, goggles, overalls, necessary for safe working with certain chemicals, etc.

personal space the immediate and intimate area around us that we consider to be our own

phalange bone in the finger or toe

pheomelanin type of melanin that creates red and yellow colour

pheromones substance secreted by the **apocrine gland** that is detected by and stimulates a response from an animal of the same species (including humans)

phosgenite rare fluorescent mineral consisting of lead chlorocarbonate

physical communication any form of communication that involves contact: primarily touching

pigment colouring matter used as a paint or dye

pigmentation excessive colouring of tissue by a pigment

plait hair style in which three lengths of hair are twisted together to create a decorative effect

plasticisers these modify polymer properties to make them more flexible and easier to wash out of the hair

polypeptides chain of amino acids, eventually form **keratin**

pore opening on the surface of the skin that allows sweat to escape

porosity test indicates the hair's condition - if the hair is smooth the cuticles are lying flat and it is in good condition

portfolio a collection of drawings or photographs of your work designed to demonstrate your talents and abilities; can be used to showcase the services you offer

posture   relevant position of parts of the body, bad posture can result in strain on muscles and ligaments and long-term problems

potassium   ingredient of relaxing hair treatment

preservatives   substances used to lengthen the life of a product

pressure test   used to test a client's sensitivity to pressure before a massage treatment

primary colours   red, blue and yellow, mixing these will give you other colours

prism   solid figure whose two ends are equilateral triangles and whose sides are rectangles; when white light is shone through a transparent figure of this shape it will break the light into the **colour spectrum**, i.e. a rainbow

professional recommendation   a suggestion to use or buy a product or service by someone who has already used it in a professional capacity

promotion   method of marketing a service or product, perhaps by reducing the price for a given period of time, or offering a special price to a particular group of people, e.g. pensioners, students, etc.

protein fibres   elastin fibres in the skin that give elasticity

proteins   essential constituent of our food, found in meat, fish, eggs, dairy products and beans and pulses

protofibrils   small bundles of cells which join together to create **microfibrils**

proton   elementary particle with positive electrical charge

prototype   a model built during research and development to test a design or invention

psoriasis   skin condition caused by the skin producing too much keratin

public liability insurance   form of insurance that must be held by all businesses to cover any claims made against the business by clients or the public (third parties) but not employees

pull test   used to assess the extent of hair loss

purified   substance that has had all impurities removed from it to make it clean

quasi permanent colour   hair colour that cannot be washed out and has to grow out

quiff   hairstyle where the hair is brushed upwards over the forehead

reception management system   IT system designed for reception

record card   completed at the consultation and updated at each visit, the record card maintains details of the client and their treatments

recycling   reusing waste items either by reprocessing them or utilising them in other ways

relaxing   the opposite of perming, removes natural curl

repetitive strain injury (RSI)   injury sustained when some parts of the body repeat certain movements

Research and Development (R&D)   the search for and evolution of new products

restructurants   ingredient of hair conditioner that penetrates the hair to repair damaged fibres in the **cortex**

reticular   dense layer of the skin next to the **basement membrane**

risk   likelihood that a hazard will actually cause harm

risk assessment   method of considering likely risks and planning to avoid them

root   part of the hair that is in the follicle

salt linkages   links holding bundles of macrofibrils together – can be broken by water; *see* **hydrogen bonds**, **sulphur bonds**

sauna   Finnish-style steam bath

sebum   the skin's natural oil, produced in the sebaceous gland

secondary colours   colours made by mixing two **primary colours**: green (blue + yellow), orange (yellow + red) and purple (red + blue)

self-employed   someone who does not have one employer (**freelance**), or someone who owns their own business

semi-permanent colour   hair colour that will last for five or six washes

senses   humans have five senses: hearing, sight, smell, taste, and touch

sensory   describing a sense or sensation; used of the nervous system

set   to style hair into waves or curls, usually by arranging wet hair as desired, often around rollers, and then drying with hot hair; the arrangement is 'set' by the heat and remains after the rollers are removed

shaft   part of the hair that is above the surface of the skin

shampoo   product used to clean hair

sharp and blunt test   used to test a client's sensitivity to sharp or blunt items

sharps   waste syringes, blades, needles, etc.; their disposal is strictly controlled

side lock of youth   tuft of hair left on the side of the shaved heads of Ancient Egyptian boys and girls who had not reached puberty

silicones   ingredient of shampoo

skeleton   hard framework of bones, cartilage, shell, etc. that supports a human or animal body

skin appendages   the collective name for the sweat glands, sebaceous glands, **hair follicles** and nails

skin test   used to test a client's sensitivity to the chemicals used in various treatments, for example hair colouring

skin toners   cleanse the skin

skull the bones that make up the cranium and the face

small and medium sized enterprises (SMEs) businesses employing less than 50 people

social identity how people place themselves into categories; how individuals relate to and connect with other individuals or groups

sodium ingredient of relaxing hair treatment

sodium sulphite prevents the colour oxidising too early in hair colouring treatments

soft water contains fewer quantities of dissolved minerals because it has passed through ground that is made up mainly of **granite**

solvents carry ingredients on to the hair and then evaporate

squoval square shaped nails which have had the corners rounded off

stance particular standing position taken up while working and performing treatments

standard industrial classification (SIC) codes a government system for classifying industries

steam vapour which water turns into when it boils

stencilling painting technique whereby colour is applied through a previously cut out shape or template

sterilised cleaned so that no micro-organisms remain

steroids any of a large group of organic compounds that includes some hormones; can be used as a drug to treat a range of conditions, but may cause unwanted hair growth, such as male pattern hair growth on women

stock taking counting the stock of consumables and non-consumables that is held by the business

story board collection of images arranged to tell a story or explain a process

strand test used to check the progress of a hair colouring treatment

styling polymers form bonds between hair strands

subculture a group within a larger group, often consisting of people drawn together by similar ideas or attitudes which may differ from those of the larger group and identified by a particular way of dressing, hairstyle or makeup

sudoriferous gland sweat-producing gland, also known as a sweat gland

sulphur bonds links holding bundles of macrofibrils together – can only be broken by chemicals; *see* **hydrogen bonds**, **salt linkages**

surface tension created by the cuticles of the hair, this prevents water absorption; shampoo breaks the surface tension, allowing the hair to be washed

surfactant an ingredient in shampoo that contains **hydrophobic** and **hydrophilic** elements and foaming agents

tactile test used to test a client's sensitivity to heat or cold

tarsals seven bones that the arch of the foot

temporary colour hair colour that will last until the next wash

tendon strong band of tissue connecting muscle to bone

tertiary colours made by mixing one primary and one secondary colour

thickeners make products such as gel and crèmes easier to apply

tibia bone of the lower leg

tone the colour you see; copper, gold, etc.

traction alopecia *see* **alopecia**

treatment liability insurance form of insurance to cover any claims made against the business by clients receiving treatments

treatment plan agreement between the therapist and the client, detailing aims, products and desired outcomes

udju green eye makeup made by the Ancient Egyptians from green malachite

ultra-violet (UV) light box box in which small tools may be sterilised or stored; ultra-violet light rays will sterilise parts of the tools they touch, so items must be turned carefully to ensure effective sterilisation

ultra-violet cabinet *see* **ultra-violet light box**

unisex style of clothing, hairstyle, etc. suitable for males and females

vacuum suction a surface treatment that removes cellular blockages and stimulates the skin's natural function

vapour moisture or other substance suspended in the air

verbal communication any form of communication that uses words: face to face conversation, telephone calls, letters, email, text, video link, etc.

visitors' book book kept at reception which should be signed by any visitors to the premises to ensure it is clear who is in the building in the event of an evacuation; clients who have made appointments do not sign the visitors' book, as the appointments book will record that they are in the building

visual aids anything a client can look at that will help you to find out what he or she wants or will allow you to show what you can offer

vitamins any of a number of elements present in many foodstuffs and essential to normal growth and functioning

vocationally related qualifications (VRQs) designed to provide candidates with skills and knowledge relevant to their chosen subject

waste management policy for dealing with all waste products; subject to local and national regulation

wrap a form of setting in which sections of hair are wrapped in cloth to create waves or curls

Index